Ominous Politics

Other books by John S. Saloma III

Congress and the New Politics

Parties: The Real Opportunity for Effective Citizen Politics
(with Frederick Sontag)

Ominous Politics

The New Conservative Labyrinth

John S. Saloma III

INTRODUCTION BY HENRY STEELE COMMAGER

A NATION BOOK

HILL and WANG · New York

A division of Farrar, Straus, and Giroux

Copyright © 1984 by Farrar, Straus and Giroux
All rights reserved

First printing, 1984

Printed in the United States of America
Published simultaneously in Canada by
Collins Publishers, Toronto
Designed by Jack Harrison

Library of Congress Cataloging in Publication Data
Saloma, John S.
  Ominous politics.
  "A Nation book."
  Bibliography: p.
  Includes index.
  1. Political participation—United States.   2. Con-
servatism—United States.   3. United States—Politics
and government—1945-   . I. Title.
JK1764.S24   1984   320.5′2′0973   83-22855
ISBN 0-8090-7295-5
ISBN 0-8090-0159-4 (pbk.)

For Charley Moore
and John Saloma

"And ye shall know the truth,
and the truth shall make you free."
John 8:32

Acknowledgments

USUALLY a book's acknowledgments are prepared by its author, but in this case that is impossible. John Saloma III, who wrote *Ominous Politics,* died in July 1983. It is left to me, the book's editor, to explain how it came to be published, and to thank some of the people who helped along the way.

Jack Saloma had for some time discussed his interest in the New Right with Hamilton Fish III, the publisher of *The Nation.* He showed Fish an early draft of a manuscript that drew on his years of research on the conservative labyrinth. Realizing its importance, Fish called it to the attention of Victor Navasky, editor of *The Nation.* Navasky determined that *Ominous Politics* should be published, and asked me to edit it. Jack Saloma witnessed my first editorial pass at the manuscript, but he never saw the finished work.

Shortly before Saloma died, I was able to give him the good news that Arthur Wang had accepted *Ominous Politics* for publication. He was extremely gratified to know that his book would appear under Wang's distinguished imprint. Working with Arthur Wang has been a personal pleasure for me and a collective good fortune for us all. Publishers of his intelligence, energy, and generosity are rare.

Several other people made important contributions to *Ominous Politics.* Shirley Sulat's typing of the first edited manuscript was as heroic as it was accurate—for reasons she and I know very well. Jerome Cobb, a *Nation* intern in the summer of 1983, was a cheerful and indefatigable researcher and fact-checker, always willing to make one more call. On Jack Saloma's end, David C. Miller helped with the preparation of the manuscript. And Saloma's friend Tanya Melich, a political consultant, kindly shared with me the story of Jack's first experience with the New Right.

I hope that all of our efforts have resulted in the most effective possible presentation of Saloma's last testament. Ultimately, as Saloma wrote in his Foreword, "there is inevitably a risk of error in attempting to tell this remarkable story without access to the inner sanctums where the actual decisions are reached."

Elsa Dixler
October 1983

Contents

Introduction

Professor Saloma's introduction to "conservative" politics came
as president of the long-outmoded Ripon Society: it was, he
confesses, at once an edifying and a disillusioning experience.
What he offers us in his analysis are not only reflections upon
his own experience but, of far broader interest, a graphic and
almost dramatic diagram of institutions which constitute a "new"
order. "I became familiar," he tells us, "with the Goldwater
brain trust supplied by the American Enterprise Institute, the
zealots of the Young Americans for Freedom, and the well-
financed ideologues of the John Birch Society working at the
grass-roots level."

Saloma calls the miscellaneous aggregation of special interest
(special fear, special prejudice, special animosity) groups, whose
anatomy he here dissects, a "new political order." His book
makes clear that a more appropriate description would be the
"new political disorder."

That disorder is, to put it quite simply, the product of money
in politics. What must concern not only all students but all
participants in our political system is why we have permitted
this disorder to infect our political system.

Few Americans realize that the problem of "money in
politics" is no problem at all in our sister democracies in Western
Europe or the British Commonwealth. Few remember that it is
relatively new even in the United States. Presidential candidates,
from Washington (who had to borrow one hundred dollars to
go to New York for his Inauguration) to Lincoln, and from

Grant to Cleveland, did not spend money on campaigns, nor, aside from dispensing refreshments and arranging torch-lit parades, did the parties. Somehow we managed for over a hundred years to get our Presidents (and most of our congressmen) on the cheap, as it were, and most of them turned out to be rather more honorable and more effective than those we buy today. It was Mark Hanna who, in 1896, confronted with the dire threat from that

Prairie Avenger, Mountain Lion
Bryan, Bryan, Bryan, Bryan
Smashing Plymouth Rock with his boulders from the West

was able to raise millions (perhaps as many as fifteen) from panicky corporations and right-minded Conservatives to install William McKinley in the White House and thus save the Republic from ruin.

Innocence once lost could not be regained. With each presidential and congressional election the cost of victory went up. (As I write, Governor Edwards has won Louisiana with a campaign fund of thirteen million!) It is now prohibitive for all but multimillionaires or those who are prepared to embrace their benefactors.

Clearly, if we do not find some way to take money out of politics, money will corrupt politics and in the end democracy itself. That process is already under way.

The first victim will be the political party.

Americans invented the modern political party and, from the beginning, imposed on that invention three attributes which have enabled it to function effectively, with only one exception, for almost two hundred years. What were those attributes and why is it so important that parties retain them? First, parties emerged, in the 1790s, as a two-party, not a multi-party, system— a phenomenon unique to the English-speaking peoples, and one which proclaims and dramatizes a genius for pragmatism and for compromise. Second, we created parties that grew up from below, rather than down from above (as in nineteenth-century aristocratic and twentieth-century totalitarian states), and that were, therefore, "democratic." Third, and not least important, we created parties which, until the fateful election of 1860, eschewed ideologies or fundamental philosophical or religious differences, and chose instead to concentrate on winning elections and running the government. This was possible because, except on the slavery issue—which became a Union issue— Americans were not divided by ideological commitments. This has been the American way of circumventing those sectional, class, ethnic, religious, and economic rivalries which, in a nation the size of fifteen Western European nations and with as many racial, religious, and class distinctions as all of them, might otherwise have threatened unremitting internal rivalries and hostilities. This was achieved not only by avoiding ideological differences but by creating parties each of which was a pretty representative cross-section of the whole people. Americans made their parties not so much the soul or even the brain but the nervous system of the constitutional framework.

What Professor Saloma makes clear is that we are now in danger of abandoning or repudiating this essential feature of our political system and creating what we have heretofore escaped: factions that are designed to represent irreconcilable political, economic, and even moral philosophies. In tracing the power and functioning of almost wholly unregulated special-interest groups, Saloma demonstrates how these subsidize and in some respects are themselves those very "factions" against which Washington warned in his Farewell Address. To be sure, our two traditional parties are also made up of a network of factions, but those factions have, historically, represented geography or tradition, or been comprised of personal followers. They have not been ideological. The new "conservative" network is self-righteously ideological: it links together and coordinates neo-conservatives, neo-liberals, military-corporate interests, the disciples of that Social Darwinism which was discredited a century ago, rapt irredentists of the Confederacy who still cling to the fantasy of states' rights, and religious and moral fundamentalists who are confident that they represent the will of God.

These new "factions," disguising themselves (perhaps even to themselves) as merely political-action committees, while similar to those factions feared by the Founding Fathers differ from them in three respects. First, in the vast sums of money they command, and dispense, without either supervision or accounting. Second, in the complicated mechanisms and institutions through which they function. The third difference is one for which the New Right has no responsibility but which—because they command such vast resources—operates greatly to their advantage: television.

Television, to be sure, flourishes in every major nation. Only in the United States and, perhaps, the Soviet Union and other totalitarian nations is it the darling of powerful economic and corporate interests, or of the government. Doubtless, television's sponsors consider their contribution to our political education benign, rather than malign. They enable candidates for public office to address the whole people as never before in history; on the other hand, they, rather than the electorate, set the terms for these hearings. Inevitably, those terms favor the big spenders. If we cannot say that to the victors belong the spoils, we can increasingly say that to the spoilsmen belong the victories.

The problem of television's impact upon our political system is not merely that of the money it commands; it is equally one of prestige and power. For candidates and parties have, astonishingly enough, acquiesced in the authority of television to stage its own shows, select the journalists to ask the questions, limit the responses of the candidates to two or three minutes, and provide its own commentators to bring in the verdict. Imagine a Lincoln or a Douglas, a Churchill, a de Gaulle, an F.D.R. submitting to this indignity!

All this is implicit in Professor Saloma's exhaustive analysis of the threat to American democracy from well-heeled special-interest groups whose activities are both government-free and fancy-free. Had Mr. Saloma lived, he would doubtless have made explicit that the most urgent task before those who cherish Jefferson's admonition that "the will of the majority is in all cases to prevail, but that will to be rightful must be reasonable" is to repudiate the subversion of Reason by money.

Henry Steele Commager

Foreword

THE THESIS of *Ominous Politics* is simple but dramatic: Over a period of more than two decades, political conservatives have quietly built a vast coalition of think tanks, political action groups, religious broadcasters, corporate political organizations, senators and representatives, Republican Party officials, and other groups with budgets totaling hundreds of millions of dollars annually. I emphasize the word "quietly" because this major development in American politics has not been much discussed in the media, or been the subject of serious study and publication. It has arrived almost unannounced.

Conservatives have largely succeeded in building institutions that incorporate a new long-term strategic dimension into American politics. The high level of organizational development has given political conservatism a decisive advantage over poorly organized liberals in the 1980s. It is impossible to know how events will unfold, but the title of this book, *Ominous Politics,* represents my concern.

My unusual background may have predisposed me to perceive the organizational interconnections and historical roots of this new political order, that is, its foundation or basic framework, earlier than most observers. While completing my education at MIT and Harvard in the 1950s and early 1960s, I became fascinated with American government and politics. (My graduate degree was a double major in political economy and government.) I spent several summers in Washington as a graduate intern in the executive branch and was fortunate to be selected a Congressional Fellow of the American Political Science Association during the academic year 1961–62. Thus began my exposure to congressional and partisan politics.

Political scientists, as a rule, try to maintain a clinical detachment from their subject matter. They may form warm associations with political actors, but there is an unwritten taboo against becoming involved in politics as a participant. (The researcher's strategy of "participant observation" allows a degree of participation, but only as a neutral observer.) Such a role did not suit me well. To discover how politics really worked, I had to cross the line and participate. I began working in Washington with the nucleus of moderate House Republicans that later became the Wednesday Group.

In September 1962, I returned to the academic world for what was to be a ten-year stint on the MIT political science faculty. Still the participant, I considered running for Congress as a liberal Republican from my home district, but soon became disillusioned with party organization politics in the Bay State. Instead, I invested my energies in consulting with Republicans in Congress, and in December 1962, I co-founded and became the first president of the Ripon Society. This progressive Republican research and policy group, named for the birthplace of the Republican Party, was initially based in Cambridge.

Meanwhile, Republican conservatives were quietly mobilizing the Draft Goldwater movement, taking over one state organization after another. The Ripon network of young professors, law and graduate students, and professionals worked quietly until the Kennedy assassination in November 1963 and the dramatic Goldwater campaign in 1964.

Suddenly the society and its leaders were thrust onto the stage of national politics. The January 1964 Ripon manifesto, "A Call to Excellence in Leadership," and its joint policy statement on civil rights with the Republican Citizens Committee, gained national attention. While the society strongly opposed the ideological emphasis and direction of Goldwater conservatism and the radical right, it endorsed no Republican presidential candidate in 1964. Individual members worked in various primary campaigns. I joined Governor William Scranton of Pennsylvania as a speechwriter and was in San Francisco for Goldwater's nomination—a watershed event in contemporary politics.

Ripon had correctly forecast an electoral disaster for the Republicans if Goldwater was nominated and later published a lengthy state-by-state analysis of the November returns. Following the election, the society joined the bitter struggle for the future direction of the Republican Party, working with groups like the newly organized Republican Governors Association.

Involvement in these events gave me a firsthand education in conservative politics and strategy, and an almost instinctive feel for the conservative style of political operation. I became familiar with the Goldwater brain trust supplied by the American Enterprise Institute (AEI), the zealots of the Young Americans for Freedom, and the well-financed ideologues of the John Birch Society working at the grass-roots level. It was an experience both frightening and sobering—a baptism by fire that few political scientists or Washington correspondents shared. It laid a foundation from which to observe and interpret political developments over the next two decades.

In February 1967, I resigned as president of the Ripon Society to devote full time to research, writing, and teaching, but continued to follow national politics closely. I completed a book on Congress (*Congress and the New Politics*, Little, Brown, 1969) and was co-author of one on party modernization (*Parties: The Real Opportunity for Effective Citizen Politics*, Knopf, 1972). It was based on three years of interviews with party leaders across the nation and intensive research into contemporary political developments, including political consulting. This non-partisan analytical work gave me perspective on the long-term trends that were shaping the political system. My interest in conservative politics became secondary, although *Parties* contains a brief account of conservative activities as of 1972.

By 1974, I had decided to pursue new research interests in California, including the increasingly significant "consciousness movement." I maintained an active interest in American politics, teaching at San Francisco State and other California universities. In 1979, I joined the faculty of the Executive MBA program at Saint Mary's College in Moraga, and learned about the new field of business and society.

It may be that some detachment from politics and distance from the political world of the Northeast made it possible for me to see the developments described in *Ominous Politics*. I tried to communicate my concern to friends and associates, but few accepted my interpretation. I began to realize that I had witnessed critical connecting events over a number of years. Indeed, most Washington observers still do not appreciate the significance of what has happened and is happening.

During the first two years of the Reagan Administration, liberals sensed they were on the defensive in a new way, especially as the President gained bipartisan majorities in Congress for his economic programs. Since the 1982 elections, however, the urgency seems to have passed. Conventional wisdom has it that the conservative challenge has been turned back. New Right political action committees like the National Conservative Political Action Committee (NCPAC) and Jesse Helms's Congressional Club lost almost every race they entered (although they raised an estimated $9 million and $10 million respectively in campaign funds). The President lost his conservative ideological majority in the House, while the New Right social program bogged down in the Senate. The *status quo ante* seemed to have returned.

But we must not mistake a shift in electoral fortunes for a political trend. Republican losses in 1982, considering that the unemployment rate was 10 percent, were surprisingly small. We need to turn our perspective upside down—to focus on the issues and procedures the conservatives have changed, rather than on electoral outcomes. The conservative labyrinth is a major new presence in American politics, not simply a short-term phenomenon. Any serious discussion of the politics of the 1980s must confront this fact.

This book attempts to present the conservative movement in a broader perspective. The reader will quickly recognize, for example, that the same names appear again and again, reflecting and creating ties among organizations. Seemingly unrelated developments take on new significance when viewed as part of a broad strategy. Taking the catalogues, annual reports, and publications of the full range of conservative organizations, cutting them up by policy field or political function, and correlating them across organizations, one can anticipate the public policy debates and political strategy of the years ahead.

Ominous Politics is based on a variety of sources, personal and public. The discussion of conservative activists, conservatives in Congress, and Republican politics comes from my own experience. A careful reading of several daily newspapers provided useful pieces of the story. I have carefully read the fund-raising brochures, magazines, and other documents published by conservative organizations. In addition, because premier think tanks like the Hoover Institution and the Institute for Contemporary Studies are based in the Bay Area, a steady stream of conservative leaders passes through San Francisco, where I live, raising funds and disseminating information to friendly public audiences.

The most helpful published sources are included in a list of selected references, although it has been almost impossible to footnote adequately my file of newspaper accounts gathered over seven years. I have chosen not to interrupt the flow of the narrative with footnotes. In many cases, the source of information is identified in the text. When it is not, the reader can find it by consulting the bibliography.

The conservatives have always been careful to allow only the most trusted into their inner circles, and there is inevitably a risk of error in attempting to tell this remarkable story without access to the inner sanctums where the actual decisions are reached. Ideally, one of the insiders should chronicle the events summarized here, but it may be years before that happens. Still, I am convinced of the general accuracy of this account, and I am confident that further research will confirm and extend the picture I have presented.

Ominous Politics

1

Charting the
Conservative Labyrinth

MOST of the self-identified conservatives interpret the label as
strongly ideological. The term describes the Taft and McCarthy
Republicans of the 1950s and the Goldwater and Reagan Republicans of the 1960s, who rejected much of the New Deal
social and economic philosophy, not to mention the interna-
tionalist outlook of the traditional Eastern Republican establishment. The ideological dimension of conservatism was most
clearly expressed in the Goldwater movement of 1960–64 and
has been muted for strategic reasons since the Reagan gubernatorial campaign of 1965–66 in California.

As the conservative coalition broadened over the 1960s and
1970s, other emphases and issues evolved. But a core of conservative activists and intellectuals have continued to control
key organizations and to set the ideological tone of the network—people like William Rusher of the *National Review*,
M. Stanton Evans of the *Indianapolis News*, and Phyllis
Schlafly of the Stop ERA movement. The "better dead than
Red" anti-Communism of the Goldwater period still serves, in
more sophisticated and intellectually respectable form, as the
ideological cement of the neoconservative/conservative Democratic alliance. The Goldwater assault on New Deal social and
economic policy, intellectually guided by Milton Friedman

and a much-less-apologetically "conservative" American Enterprise Institute, has become (after the excesses of the programs enacted under the Great Society) a philosophical attack on uncontrolled government spending, excessive regulation, and the evils of bureaucracy.

The story of the rise of the conservative labyrinth still remains largely untold. A feature issue of *Esquire* (February 1979) devoted to neoconservatism, for example, included a two-page chart of the "neoconservative establishment," somewhat tongue-in-cheek, emphasizing personalities rather than organizations. The first article, to my knowledge, to portray the wide scope and serious intent of the conservative effort was written by *Washington Post* staff writer Dan Morgan and appeared on January 4, 1981. Morgan compiled data on "an extensive and well-financed network of think tanks in Washington and New York, national magazines, organizations that crank out research on dozens of public policy issues or spread the conservative message on campuses, and activist legal groups that help corporations fight government regulation." Accompanying the article was a chart of "the conservative network," covering almost a full page. It displayed some seventy organizations in more than a dozen categories, ranging from national security/foreign policy to legislation, media, and campus outreach. Donors identified included nine conservative foundations and more than a score of major corporations.

In the pages that follow, I have filled in many of the details that Morgan's broad picture only suggested. Each of the next twelve chapters is devoted to a major sector of the conservative infrastructure. Here, I will provide an overview, a rough map of the conservative labyrinth.

The conservative think tanks, which emphasize research and publication that is essentially "above politics," form a clearly identifiable group of organizations, and our journey begins with them. They are funded in large part by conservative foundations, to which I next turn. Another important group of organizations is specifically devoted to political action and electoral politics. Since 1974, its core has been a cluster of New Right organizations, financed largely by direct mail. These organizations are supported and amplified by the fundamentalist religious right and its impressive communications network. The political and the religious groups are each the subject of a chapter.

Perhaps even more important and less visible is the substantial investment of corporate America since the mid-1970s in political action committees, grass-roots political organization, and teaching about free enterprise, often in cooperation with the conservative think tanks and political action committees. This, too, receives notice.

The major institutions of national politics, Congress and the political parties, are also foci for conservative influence. Individuals like Senator Jesse Helms have used their offices to build unprecedented extra-congressional organizations. Conservatives move in and out of the Republican Party, using their positions in party organizations to strengthen their movement. Congressional conservatives and the Republican Party are each the subject of a chapter.

Completing this picture of the conservative labyrinth are several more specialized groups. Conservative Democrats have been courted by the right and recruited into bipartisan organizations in support of its domestic and foreign policies. The rise of the Libertarian Party complements the growth of the network. A chapter is devoted to both these phenomena. The preoccupation with the media shared by most conservative groups has generated extensive public-relations campaigns, independent television programming, and well-financed monitoring operations. They receive a chapter, as do the conservative public-interest law firms and research organizations set up to counter the movement concerned with consumer and environmental affairs. Finally, the effort to build a conservative black political movement warrants a chapter. Concluding chapters examine the history of the conservative labyrinth and the question of how moderates and liberals can most appropriately respond to it.

This journey through the conservative labyrinth is necessarily selective and incomplete. For every organization I discuss, I could just as well have selected another. Every one is well funded and staffed and runs a full complement of programs. Conservatives have built deeply as well as broadly; instead of funding one or two major think tanks, for example, they have created dozens. And the network is still growing. New organizations and programs continue to emerge, suggesting a development plan stretching well into the 1980s.

An investment of this scale and duration suggests serious intent. The conservatives have laid the groundwork and expect to govern this country for decades. This book both describes that effort and attempts to suggest how it can be stopped.

2

Think Tanks and Thinkers: We Write the Songs

THE CONSERVATIVE THINK TANKS are the most impressive evidence of strategic planning by the conservatives. As recently as the late 1950s, a Washington joke defined a Republican brain trust as "Malcolm Moos with mirrors." By 1964, the conservatives (no friends of Moos, a liberal Republican political scientist who served in the Eisenhower White House), had mobilized a small band of conservative intellectuals through AEI and the Hoover Institution to form a brain trust for Goldwater. In the mid-1960s, prominent conservatives like Melvin Laird and David Packard were actively raising funds for Hoover and for an AEI spinoff, the Georgetown Center for Strategic and International Studies (CSIS). By 1979, when William Simon published his manifesto, *A Time for Truth*, with its ringing call for the creation of a "conservative counterintelligentsia" as the only effective challenge to liberal domination of media, foundations, and universities, most of the conservative think tanks were already at work.

The conservative think tank is a good place to begin a deeper look at the conservative labyrinth. Journalistic comparisons to the Brookings Institution (as "the Democratic administration in exile") and the leftist Institute for Policy Studies in Washington are not accurate; conservative think tanks are something new in American politics. Each has developed its own policy emphases and specialties, and each generates a variety of political initiatives. They are much better funded than their liberal predecessors and much more closely tied to the government administration. A closer examination of three of the think tanks—AEI, the Institute for Contemporary Studies, and the Heritage Foundation—illustrates the diversity of their activities.

The AEI motto, "Competition of ideas is fundamental to a free society," hints at the connection between policy research and the contemporary political agenda. The late William Baroody, Sr., who brought AEI to its current stature, had a keen sense of the value of timely ideas in politics, and he and others were able to sell this insight effectively to corporate executives and foundation directors. The AEI publications catalogue lists a staggering array of monographs and books that anticipate emerging issues and policy debates.

AEI does more than commission research through its 145 resident scholars, fellows, and staff, and over 80 adjunct scholars. Since the early 1960s, it has developed perhaps the most effective public-relations campaign for disseminating political ideas that has ever been mounted. AEI directs a steady flow of editorial-page articles to some 100 daily newspapers in the United States. Its televised *Public Policy Forums*, covering more than 100 separate topics since 1970, were aired on 600 television, CATV, and radio stations across the country in 1982. More than 100 AEI publications are annually made available to AEI-sponsored Public Policy Research Centers in more than 200 American colleges and universities. In 1982, AEI budgeted $2.6 million out of a total of $11.7 million for public outreach alone.

I can testify personally to the effective, long-term public-relations strategy of AEI. In the early 1960s, AEI commissioned me to prepare a monograph on the congressional budget process. AEI, under investigation by the IRS, must have found it advantageous to have a known liberal Republican among its authors. Subsequently, AEI arranged a feature article about my work on the *Los Angeles Times* business page, republication of the monograph in testimony about the Congressional Budget and Impoundment Control Act of 1974, and an invitation for me to testify on the new legislation before the House Rules Committee.

A sense of the political clout of AEI is conveyed by its strategy for recruiting fellows, its independent publication of magazines, and the development strategy it has. Two of AEI's senior fellows have been instrumental in building the neoconservative/conservative Democratic network in the intellectual community: Irving Kristol, who has been called the "Godfather" of the neoconservative movement, and Ben Wattenberg, cofounder and co-chairman of the Coalition for a Democratic Majority. Kristol, as co-editor of *The Public Interest*, a neoconservative journal, and a member of the Board of Contributors to the editorial page of *The Wall Street Journal*, is in an excellent position to disseminate new ideas. Wattenberg has been the host of a major public television broadcast series funded by a consortium of conservative foundations and corporations.

AEI scholars have connections with the major media. Norman J. Ornstein consulted with CBS News on the 1982 Senate races; Richard M. Scammon continued his fifteen-year association with NBC News on election night that year; and Howard R. Penniman has advised ABC News since 1960. AEI has also courted the nation's political science establishment by appointing influential members of the American Political Science Association as Resident Scholars: Jeane Kirkpatrick (wife of recently retired APSA executive director Evron M. Kirkpatrick, who now has an office at AEI), currently on leave as ambassador to the UN; Howard Penniman; and Austin Ranney. AEI's publications on the American and other political systems have increased dramatically.

In 1977, AEI began publishing its own periodicals: *Public Opinion, Regulation, AEI Foreign Policy and Defense Review,* and *The AEI Economist.* The most impressive of these magazines is *Public Opinion.* Occupying a position between the professional public-opinion journals, with their limited readership, and the Gallup and Harris polls that appear in the daily press, *Public Opinion* has carved out an influential audience. The magazine commissions articles from almost every American political pollster and public-opinion analyst, as well as from many overseas. Its "Opinion Roundup" section summarizes the latest public-opinion data with sophisticated graphics.

AEI's development plan includes the funding of study centers, projects, and endowed chairs. By the time Reagan took office, five AEI centers were functioning (Center for the Study of Government Regulation; Economic Policy; Political and Social Processes; Legal Policy; and Religion, Philosophy, and Public Policy), as well as five smaller projects on health policy, Congress, defense policy, foreign policy, and the Constitution. (AEI annual reports refer to other projects and do not distinguish between centers and projects. The listing here is therefore partial.) An AEI Development Committee including Gerald R. Ford, Reginald H. Jones of General Electric, Thomas A. Murphy of General Motors, Walter B. Wriston of Citicorp/Citibank, Willard C. Butcher of Chase Manhattan, and Irving Kristol has been seeking major capital commitments (an endowment) of $60 million from individuals, families, corporations, and foundations. (Hoover already has raised a $40 million endowment and Georgetown CSIS has three $2 million chairs as part of its endowment.) The AEI Development Committee has asked for capital grants of $10 million for centers, $5 million for projects, and pledges of $1 million for designated chairs. At least five AEI chairs have already been endowed by the Potlatch Corporation, the Weyerhaeuser Company Foundation, the Reader's Digest Foundation, the Ford Motor Company Fund, and the John M. Olin Foundation.

One AEI interest deserves special note, the Center for the Study of Religion, Philosophy, and Public Policy and the related fields of democratic capitalism and mediating structures (families, churches, neighborhood groups, voluntary associations, and ethnic subgroupings). AEI resident scholar Michael Novak (assisted by adjunct scholars like Peter Berger at Boston College) has been pivotal in AEI's theological and religious outreach program. Novak's columns appear regularly in the *National Catholic Reporter* and he is active in the Catholic League for Religious and Civil Rights. I was impressed to find an AEI publications booth at an annual Conference of Biblical Scholars in San Francisco several years ago.

This World, the latest AEI spinoff publication, is published in association with another organization based in New York, the Institute for Educational Affairs. (The institute, a foundation created by William E. Simon and Irving Kristol, has dispensed more than $2.5 million in grants to academics since 1979. *The New York Times* notes that the institute also serves "as a kind of middleman, or adviser, to smaller companies that want to provide grants," a source totaling about $2 million in 1981.)

The purposes of "the critics, scholars, and churchmen" who are launching *This World* are, they claim, "to restate, in contemporary terms, the moral values that undergird our society; to assert their relevance to the political, economic, and cultural issues of our time; and, by the force of superior logic, to uphold them against self-serving and uninformed assaults." Novak co-edits the high-budget intellectual journal. One final example will illustrate the affluence of AEI. The major annual "event" at AEI is a week-long series of public-policy forums, panels, and black-tie dinners. The price tag for the 1982 AEI week, according to *The New York Times*, was "well over $100,000."

While AEI is an impressive flagship, the conservatives have an entire fleet. A different format has been developed by the San Francisco-based Institute for Contemporary Studies (ICS). ICS was founded in 1972, near the close of the second Reagan administration in California, by a group of his advisers, including Edwin Meese III and ICS president H. Monroe Browne. After President Reagan appointed Browne ambassador to New Zealand in 1981, he was succeeded at ICS by Dr. Glenn S. Dumke, former chancellor of the California State University system. ICS is a comparatively small operation, with seven full-time and four part-time employees and a budget in the range of $1.2 million. The institute specializes in book-length public-policy studies that can be edited and rushed into print in 90 to 180 days. The institute also publishes a quarterly *Journal of Contemporary Studies* (formerly *Taxing and Spending*). The typical ICS book is a compilation of original articles commissioned by a project editor assisted by the institute staff. *The Economy in the 1980s* (June 1980), edited by Michael J. Boskin, a professor of economics at Stanford, and *National Security in the 1980s* (May 1980), edited by W. Scott Thompson from the Fletcher School at Tufts, are representative. Two ICS volumes drew national attention early in the Reagan Administration. *Politics and the Oval Office*, edited by Arnold J. Meltsner of the University of California at Berkeley, was widely regarded as a primer in White House politics for the new administration. Even more significant was *The Fairmont Papers*, the proceedings of a Black Alternatives Conference at the Fairmont Hotel in San Francisco in December 1980, organized by Thomas Sowell of Stanford and ICS. The conference was a conscious effort to provide the new administration with alternative (distinctively "conservative") policies to those of the liberal civil-rights establishment and to encourage the establishment of new national organizations for black alternatives.

Another example of its involvement in strategic issue development for the conservatives was the September 1981 ICS conference on the "new federalism" held at the Mayflower Hotel in Washington, D.C. The conference was chaired by Robert B. Hawkins of the Sequoia Institute (Sacramento, California), a former Reagan gubernatorial aide on local government who advises the Reagan Administration on intergovernmental relationships. Other top-level participants in the conference were Senator Paul Laxalt of Nevada and veteran Republican political strategist F. Clifton White. (Laxalt heads a 41-member advisory commission on federalism set up by Reagan in April 1981. White is one of five private citizens named to the commission.) After Reagan's January 1982 proposals on the new federalism, the John M. Olin Foundation and the Institute for Educational Affairs—two major funding sources in the infrastructure—gave $24,000 to "the first nationwide symposium on federalism" sponsored at Yale University by a new conservative student organization, the Yale Federalist Society.

The ICS meeting in February 1983 included panels on Reaganomics, nuclear arms, world economic growth, and United States strategy vis-à-vis the Soviet Union. Featured speakers at the meeting included Edwin Meese III, California governor George Deukmejian, and British MP Eldon Griffiths. ICS also sponsors a bimonthly business and government roundtable which "provides a forum for leaders of business, government, and academia to meet and exchange views on important contemporary policy issues."

The ICS model illustrates how effectively the conservatives have recruited and supported younger academics and intellectuals, maintained a conservative/neoconservative network within the university community, and related policy research to contemporary politics. The success of the new conservative intelligentsia rests at least as much on this skillful "networking" as it does on AEI's institution building. (ICS has also developed an international network. The institute recently published a comparative study of social-security systems in eight industrialized countries with the Fondation Nationale d'Economie Politique in Paris.)

The sudden rise and distinctive new role of the Heritage Foundation is somewhat unusual among conservative think tanks. Formed by Joseph Coors and New Right political strategist Paul Weyrich in 1973 with a gift of $250,000 from Coors (and a large contribution from Richard Scaife), the Heritage Foundation now has an annual budget of over $10 million. The Coors-Weyrich axis, discussed later in the section on conservative political action groups, has generally been regarded as strongly New Right. *New Republic* columnist Morton Kondracke describes Heritage as "a committed rightist organization" which is "ideologically distinct from the establishment think tanks of the right and left." "Anything to the right of the Heritage is the fringe," comments an official of one of the traditional think tanks. Burton Pines of Heritage draws the following contrast with AEI: "AEI is like the big gun on an offshore battleship. We are the landing party. If they hadn't softened it up, we wouldn't have landed." Journalist Sidney Blumenthal adds: "Ideas are its instruments for power. It wants not only to manufacture beliefs, but also to dominate government." The Heritage Foundation has come to play the powerful role of overseeing—almost like a "shadow government"—the Reagan Administration.

The ultraconservative origins of Heritage are reflected in its board of trustees: Coors, California industrialist J. Robert Fluor, former Treasury Secretary William E. Simon, Midge Decter, the author and executive director of the Committee for the Free World, and Lewis Lehrman, president of the Rite-Aid Corporation, who was the unsuccessful Republican candidate for governor of New York in 1982, industrialist Robert Krieble, former U.S. Information Agency head Frank Shakespeare, former Reagan California aide Frank J. Walton, and drugstore entrepreneur Jack Eckerd. The past board chairman is Ben B. Blackburn, a former Republican member of Congress from Georgia with a strong anti-civil-rights voting record. Shakespeare recently replaced him in that post. Also prominent in building Heritage has been Edward E. Noble, Oklahoma oil and gas tycoon and current chairman of the Synthetic Fuels Corporation. Edwin J. Feulner, Jr.—recruited by representatives of Richard Scaife, according to David Warner of the Pittsburgh *Post-Gazette*—became its president in April 1977.

The Heritage Foundation gained public visibility in November 1980 during the Reagan transition. Working out of the foundation's white brick row houses northeast of the Capitol— replaced in 1983 by a $9.5 billion beige brick building overlooking Capitol Hill—about 250 congressional aides, former Republican Administration officials, and academics prepared an unprecedented 3,000-page, 20-volume report entitled *Mandate for Leadership: Policy Management in a Conservative Administration.* (A 1,000-page paperback edition sold for $12.95, and was on the *Washington Post* best-seller list for three weeks at the start of the new administration.) What made this effort so unusual was that the Reagan team had already mounted the most organized, sophisticated, and highly structured official transition in American history, supplementing public funds with tax-exempt private contributions. The Heritage transition report, with an announced budget of $100,000, was publicized as "a blueprint for conservative government." No private group not officially associated with an incoming President had ever presented such a detailed plan for taking over the reins of government. The document was received for the President by Edwin Meese III, the director of the Reagan transition team, with a public endorsement, an event covered by TV network evening news.

The blueprint included recommendations for cutting government bureaucracy and building up the defense establishment. The Heritage position came through most clearly in the call for the abolition of many restrictions on domestic intelligence work and for the renewal of congressional panels on "internal security." The study advised Reagan to recognize "the reality of subversion and [to put] emphasis on the un-American nature of much so-called dissidence." "It is axiomatic," the study noted, "that individual liberties are secondary to the requirement of national security and internal civil order." *Mandate* was conceived by Feulner, Blackburn, and Shakespeare in the fall of 1979, before it was clear who the Republican nominee would be.

While the official Reagan transition team was dissolved when the new President took office, Heritage has continued to monitor the Reagan Administration. A typical example is the 16-page analysis of the Department of Interior, prepared by Robert L. Terrell of Heritage as part of *Mandate for Leadership* and circulated to the department's staff by then-Secretary James Watt with the endorsement: "Many of his comments deserve serious consideration." Heritage also played a role in the removal of Education Department undersecretary William C. Clohan, Jr. Feulner claimed in March 1982 that the Reagan Administration had adopted 61 percent of the 1,270 recommendations included in *Mandate.* Heritage has issued a follow-up progress report on the Reagan government entitled *The First Year.*

The Washington establishment has gained increasing respect for the Heritage apparatus and its influence within the Reagan high command. Feulner served on the Reagan transition executive committee (fourteen other Heritage staff and board members also had transition appointments) but declined to join the administration. Instead, Meese has made him a consultant on policy, and he chairs the Advisory Commission on Public Diplomacy, which oversees the U.S. International Communication Agency. The Heritage-Reagan Administration connection was dramatically illustrated when Meese endorsed Heritage's new President's Club. For a tax-deductible donation of $1,000 or more, selected conservative contributors are offered, in Feulner's words, "access to Washington policymakers which cannot be had at any price."

Heritage has won respectability without compromising its conservative ideological commitment. Economist Milton Friedman and publisher William Buckley, Jr., addressed a gala banquet in May 1980. The foundation's list of scholars and fellows has included conservative author Russell Kirk; Soviet specialist Robert Conquest; the late Herman Kahn, director of the Hudson Institute; and neoconservative author Midge Decter and her husband, Norman Podhoretz, editor of *Commentary* magazine, among others. The Heritage journal, *Policy Review,* edited by John O'Sullivan, former assistant editor of the *London Daily Telegraph,* has featured such neoconservatives and conservative Democrats as Senator Daniel Patrick Moynihan, Eugene V. Rostow, and former Humphrey aide Max M. Kampelman.

Heritage has a full-time staff of 90, including 30 in-house research analysts, young Ph.D.s or Ph.D. candidates who draw annual salaries of $15,000 to $25,000. In addition to producing timely research analyses, the staff assist in the publication of more than a half dozen monthly reports and newsletters, including *Institution Analysis*, which examines the affiliations and histories of individuals and groups of the political left. One Heritage project in particular highlights the foundation's unique role in the infrastructure—its Resource Bank. Headed by senior vice president Willa Ann Johnson, former deputy director of the personnel office of the Reagan White House, the Resource Bank is comprised of a network of some 450 research groups and 1,600 scholars and public-policy experts. Heritage devotes approximately 15 percent of its budget, over $1 million of its 1982 funds, to what Johnson describes as "a clearinghouse, a conduit, and a catalyst." "For the first time," she observes, "there is a broadly conservative policy network actively operating on a national basis." Morton Kondracke concludes that Heritage produces little original research but is "astoundingly good at packaging and trumpeting conservative proposals in the media." (The foundation claims credit for the policy concept of urban "enterprise zones" developed by Heritage economist Stuart M. Butler, but the idea is British in origin.) "Heritage gets at least as much press attention as AEI," Kondracke states, an amazing feat considering its smaller budget and more recent origin.

Like AEI, Heritage draws important support from the Fortune 500. (Feulner claims that 87 of the top corporations contribute. A *National Journal* profile lists Chase Manhattan Bank N.A., Mobil Oil Corporation, Smith Kline Corporation, Fluor Corporation, Reader's Digest Association, Inc., Gulf Oil Corporation and G. D. Searle and Company among the largest corporate contributors, as well as the Olin Foundation and the Noble Foundation.) It is unique among the larger conservative think tanks, however, in having a direct-mail fund-raising base as well. Frank Walton, who served as Heritage president for a period before Feulner's appointment, introduced the direct-mail program. Today Heritage, with 122,000 financial contributors, claims to be "the most broadly based research institution in the country." The Heritage Foundation's 1982 income came from: foundations, 31 percent; individuals, 44 percent; corporations, 20 percent; interest and dividends, 3 percent; and sale of publications, 2 percent. "For the first time," Feulner adds, "you have a broadly supported think tank. We're not just Joe Coors's mouthpiece in Washington."

The Heritage Foundation remains very much in the news. It purchased time so that PBS could offer the 90-minute spectacular, "Let Poland Be Poland—A Day of Solidarity with the Polish People," produced by the U.S. International Communications Agency, to its 297 stations in January 1982. Heritage financed an investigation of the laser weapon strategy in space by a team of engineers, scientists, and international law experts, led by Lieutenant General (Retired) Daniel Grahm, the former head of Defense Intelligence. Its findings were published as *High Frontier* in March 1982. Other Heritage projects include the promotion of the concept of enterprise zones. An *Enterprise Zone News* journal is being edited by the Sabre Foundation, and a Coalition for Enterprise Zones has been organized. Some fourteen states have already passed bills calling for enterprise zones. In Connecticut, the New Haven zone is an 80-acre manufacturing site owned by Olin Corporation, a backer of conservative causes. In mid-1982, Norman B. Ture, a chief architect of the Reagan economic program, moved from the Treasury Department to Heritage as a visiting fellow and chair of the Board of Directors of the newly formed Council for Economic Advancement, a nationwide, bipartisan, grassroots effort to return the government to the basic principles of Reaganomics.

This account could just as well have focused on other conservative think tanks than AEI, ICS, and the Heritage Foundation. The Hoover Institution, for example, has become a "West Coast AEI," with senior fellows like Milton Friedman and Seymour Martin Lipset. Originally named the Hoover Institution on War, Revolution, and Peace, and founded in 1919 with a gift from Herbert Hoover "to demonstrate the evils of the doctrines of Karl Marx," it has been headed since 1960 by W. Glenn Campbell. The institution is housed in the new Herbert Hoover Memorial Building on the campus of Stanford University, built with $7 million in matching funds from the federal government. Its 1983 budget was approximately $8.4 million. Hoover's most ambitious publishing project has been *The United States in the 1980s,* an 868-page analysis of domestic and international problems by a team of social scientists. Ronald Reagan, who has a long and close association with Hoover, donated the papers of his gubernatorial administration to the institution. Another think tank, the Institute for Foreign Policy Analysis, was founded in 1976 by Robert Pfaltzgraff and stresses "the danger of international Communism and the need for a strong defense for the United States." It maintains a loose affiliation with Tufts University and has offices in Cambridge and Washington. IFPA's 1983 budget was about $1.2 million.

Other noteworthy think tanks include the Lehrman Institute of New York, which sponsors seminars in economics and foreign policy; attendance is by invitation only. Its founder is a wealthy conservative activist and entrepreneur, Lewis E. Lehrman, who spent more than $7 million of his personal fortune in an unsuccessful $11 million bid to become governor of New York in 1982. Other think tanks range from the Foreign Policy Research Institute in Philadelphia to the International Center for Economic Policy Studies in New York City, to the Lincoln Institute for Research and Education (for conservative blacks) in Washington, D.C. Even the religious right has its own think tank—the Chalcedon Institute.

Some of the self-proclaimed think tanks may exist mostly on paper, but my investigation of some small California think tanks, such as the Pacific Institute for Public Policy Research in San Francisco and the Reason Foundation in Santa Barbara, suggests that even they are staffed by competent professionals, publish quality newsletters and magazines, and have ambitious plans for conferences and publications.

There is even a conservative counterpart to the establishment Aspen Institute—the Shavano Institute for National Leadership in Keystone, Colorado. In July 1982, it announced a series of seminars for business leaders, as well as television documentaries to be broadcast over the Ted Turner cable TV network. The institute, formally a division of conservative Hillsdale College in Hillsdale, Michigan, represents, according to *The Christian Science Monitor,* "an attempt to consciously mold a new value system along the traditionally conservative lines of 'freedom, limited government, and the dignity of the individual.'" "We believe in the future, and we are doing something about it," is the way Hillsdale president George C. Roche III describes the Shavano Institute. (Some idea of the twistings and turnings of the conservative labyrinth emerges from the fact that Roche was appointed by President Reagan in June 1982 to chair the National Council on Education Research. Its members included Onalee McGraw of the Heritage Foundation, Penny Pullen of the American Legislative Exchange Council, and M. Blouke Carus, an executive of the conservative Open Court Publishers.)

The conservative think tanks form a sort of transmission belt to move ideas into politics. Devices like the Heritage Foundation resource bank bring new theories to the attention of people outside the universities. Walter Wriston, the chairman of Citicorp and a fund-raiser for AEI, points out: "It takes about twenty years for a research paper at Harvard to become a law. There weren't any people feeding the intellectual argument on the other side. . . . AEI . . . puts an idea into the market. We figured it out: I write the songs the world sings."

The rise of supply-side economics—described in detail in the next chapter—also illustrates the conservatives' capacity to bring ideas into politics. Arthur Laffer, the theorist of supply-side, claims that the academic community was prejudiced against his research. "I knew there was no way on God's earth that I could make it in the profession. So I went other routes— the press, the political process, consulting." Many of these routes were paved by think tanks, including Heritage, AEI, and Hoover. Paul Craig Roberts, another supply-sider, believes that "it is entirely possible academics would have kept supply-side economics buried in the universities for years" had it not been for the foundations and the think tanks.

Think tanks are shaping the attitudes of American voters and altering the context in which they consider issues. What they do can best be described as contextual politics. AEI's *Public Opinion* magazine and Center for Research in Advertising, the Republican National Committee consulting group on "the new rhetoric," and the public-relations campaigns of the conservative think tanks in general, have all contributed here.

Contextual politics is a brilliant and disturbing innovation because it falls outside our traditional definition of politics. Institutional advertising, designed to influence political opinion, is not completely new to American politics—conservatives used it as long ago as the last Senate campaign of Robert Taft in Ohio. What is new is the scale and sophistication. Take, for example, the campaign in California to defeat Proposition 5, the antismoking initiative, in 1978. Californians for Common Sense, the "No on 5" committee funded by a consortium of tobacco companies headed by R. J. Reynolds, spent a record $6 million to defeat the initiative. Campaign literature featured a patriot, the Liberty Bell (also the logo of the Heritage Foundation), and a scroll headed WE THE PEOPLE. Billboards and radio spots asked, "What will the regulators do next?" The underlying antiregulation message prepared voters for a whole range of issues beyond the immediate campaign.

Conservatives have appropriated powerful words and symbols—freedom, family, work, religion, common sense, patriotism—in a way that has caught the liberals unaware. Norman Lear's 1982 television special *I Love Liberty* may be the first evidence that the liberals are prepared to contest this terrain. Conservative media campaigns on issues like the Soviet arms buildup and government spending and inflation are also attempts to condition American public opinion. The think tanks provide a core of fact and the aura of respectability to these efforts.

In all these ways, conservative think tanks pursue activist agendas well beyond policy research as it has been traditionally defined or practiced by liberal think tanks. Every indication since the Reagan election is that these institutions are still growing. They are obviously a long-term investment that the conservatives expect to yield substantial returns through the 1980s into the 1990s.

3

The Foundations: Tracer Bullets

WHILE CONSERVATIVE FOUNDATIONS account for only a small portion of the funding of the labyrinth (compared to private contributions, corporate support, and direct mail), examining them illuminates its workings. Among the major foundations identified in Dan Morgan's *Washington Post* article as parts of the conservative network are: the Bechtel Foundation (construction); the Adolph Coors Foundation (brewing); the Fred C. Koch Foundation (energy, real estate); the Lilly Foundation (pharmaceuticals); the Samuel Noble Foundation (oil and drilling); the John M. Olin Foundation (agricultural chemicals, "sporting weapons"); the J. Howard Pew Freedom Trust (Sun Oil); the Smith Richardson Foundation (Vicks Vaporub); and the Sarah Mellon Scaife Foundation (Gulf Oil).

There is evidence that conservatives have given a distinct ideological cast to these as well as some smaller foundations. In 1977, William E. Simon became head of the John M. Olin Foundation of New York, and was given a free hand to reshape its grant program. In 1982, the Olin Foundation directed about $3 million to conservative research organizations. The $100 million Smith Richardson Foundation, with an annual grants budget of $3 million, also shifted to support conservative causes when R. Randolph (Randy) Richardson, son of founder H. Smith Richardson, assumed the presidency in 1973. That same year, Mellon family fortune heir Richard Scaife became chairman of the Sarah Scaife Foundation, drawing on its considerable resources to help build the New Right.

Three pieces of investigative reporting that have appeared since Reagan's election shed some light on the Scaife family foundations and the Smith Richardson Foundation. Karen Rothmyer, a former *Wall Street Journal* reporter who now teaches at the Columbia University School of Journalism, published an analysis of Richard Mellon Scaife entitled "Citizen Scaife" in the *Columbia Journalism Review* (July–August 1981). A useful profile, "Scaife: Financier of the Right," by David Warner, staff writer for the *Pittsburgh Post-Gazette*, appeared on April 29, 1981. Finally, Chris Welles, a contributing editor of *Esquire*, examined the involvement of the Smith Richardson Foundation in the "supply-side cabal" in his article "The Collapse of '84" (August 1981).

Scaife has been a major funder of the conservative movement for more than twenty years. Contributions from his private trusts to the Hoover Institution (to whose board of overseers he belongs) go back to 1962; he has been giving to the American Enterprise Institute since 1963. Rothmyer identified Scaife as "a friend from an early age of J. Edgar Hoover and a long-time admirer of Barry Goldwater." We can reasonably assume that Scaife was a member of the as yet unidentified group that helped to bankroll the Draft Goldwater movement. A 1957 *Fortune* ranking of the largest fortunes in America listed four Mellons (including Scaife's mother, Sarah Mellon Scaife) among the top eight. The income from his two trust funds, set up by his mother and totaling at least $150 million, amounts to an estimated $8 million per year. He uses a private DC-9 to travel between his residences in Pittsburgh/Ligonier, Pennsylvania, and Pebble Beach, California. After his mother's death in 1965, Scaife began exercising greater control of the four Scaife family entities: the Sarah Scaife Foundation, the Carthage Foundation, the Allegheny Foundation (which must give a public accounting of how it spends its income), and the Sarah Scaife Grandchildren's Trust (which does not). In 1973, Scaife became chairman of the Sarah Scaife Foundation. Within a year, Rothmyer reported, he broke with his sister, Cordelia Scaife May, the other heir to the Sarah Mellon Scaife fortune. Since 1965, she "had tried to restrain her brother from shifting charitable donations away from Sarah Scaife's priorities—population control and art—and toward conservative causes. After the break, she apparently gave up."

The Scaife family charitable organizations have assets of $250 million (much of it in Gulf Oil Company stock) and an annual income of at least $12 million. Rothmyer estimated that the annual donations from Scaife charities to conservative causes at the time she wrote her article amounted to about $10 million, apart from Scaife's personal contributions. The most sensitive contributions are handled by the Grandchildren's Trust, which, according to Rothmyer's private sources, now directs virtually all its funds to the conservative movement. Rothmyer estimated that the Scaife charities had donated $100 million over the past twelve years. Warner, working with different sources, concluded that "Scaife's enormously wealthy private trust funds have given $144.1 million in the past twenty-two years to a variety of organizations, many in the ideological category, and most of them politically conservative."

Rothmyer's systematic review of Scaife charitable contributions since 1973 (summarized in figure 1) revealed two further points about Scaife and the labyrinth. First, the Scaife money has been carefully targeted. "Sometimes," Rothmyer observed, "a small amount of money at the right time is of more

FIGURE I

Scaife Funding of the Infrastructure
WHERE THE MONEY GOES

Some of the larger or better-known conservative and New Right groups to which Richard Scaife gave substantial funding between 1973 and 1981 are listed below. Amounts, which include grants from the Carthage and Sarah Scaife Foundations and the Trust for the Grandchildren of Sarah Mellon Scaife, are approximate.

Defense

The Center for Strategic and International Studies, Georgetown University (Washington)	$5.3 million
Committee for the Free World (New York)*+	$50,000
Committee on the Present Danger (Washington)+	$360,000
Hoover Institution on War, Revolution, and Peace, Stanford University (Stanford)	$3.5 million
Institute for Foreign Policy Analysis (Cambridge)*+	$1.9 million
National Security Program, New York University,+ and National Strategy Information Center (New York)+	$6 million

+ *Group recently received a contribution equal to 10 percent or more of the current or most recent available budget, based on public or private records and/or confirmation by organization.*
* *Group is known to have received seed money from Scaife.*

From Karen Rothmyer, "Citizen Scaife," *Columbia Journalism Review*, July/August, 1981, p. 47. Reprinted by permission.

Economics

Foundation for Research in Economics and Education (Westwood, Calif.)	$1.4 million
International Center for Economic Policy Studies (New York) +	$150,000
International Institute for Economic Research (Westwood, Calif.)*+	$300,000
Law and Economics Center, originally at Miami University, now at Emory University (Atlanta)	$3 million
World Research, Inc. (San Diego)	$1 million

Media

Accuracy in Media (Washington)	$150,000
Alternative Educational Foundation (*The American Spectator* magazine, Bloomington, Ind.)	$900,000
The Media Institute (Washington)*+	$475,000
WQLN-TV (Erie, Pa.)	$500,000

Think Tanks

The Heritage Foundation (Washington)*+	$3.8 million
The Institute for Contemporary Studies (San Francisco)*+	$1.7 million

Political Research/Education Groups

American Legislative Exchange Council (Washington) +	$560,000
The Free Congress Research and Education Foundation, Inc. (Washington) +	$700,000

Legal Groups

Americans for Effective Law Enforcement (Evanston)	$1 million
National Legal Center for the Public Interest, plus six affiliates (Capitol Legal Foundation, Washington; Mountain States Legal Foundation, Denver; Mid-Atlantic Legal Foundation, Philadelphia; Great Plains Legal Foundation, Kansas City, Mo.; Mid-America Legal Foundation, Chicago; Southeastern Legal Foundation, Atlanta)*+	$1.8 million
Pacific Legal Foundation (Sacramento)+	$1.9 million

value than millions later on. Since 1973, Scaife entities have provided seed money to as many as two dozen New Right organizations." For example, Scaife provided $75,000 to help start the San Francisco-based Institute for Contemporary Studies in 1973. Similarly, he contributed the largest single amount of seed money ($325,000) for the Cambridge-based Institute for Foreign Policy Analysis in 1976. At about the same time, a Scaife representative delivered a check for $100,000 to the Southern California organizers of the Foundation for American Communications (FACS), who were seeking to improve relations between business and the media. (When Rothmyer wrote, FACS, yet another infrastructure organization, received about 20 percent of its $650,000 annual budget from Scaife. Besides sponsoring conferences attended by almost 500 journalists, FACS runs seminars on how to deal with the media for non-profit organizations and businesses.) Scaife helped to launch the Heritage Foundation with Joseph Coors in 1974. Scaife has remained the silent partner, initially contributing close to $900,000 (compared to $250,000 for Coors), but letting the Colorado brewer take most of the credit for organizing the foundation. Scaife has contributed as much as $1 million to Heritage in a single year, while Coors averages about $350,000. As Washington wags put it, "Coors gives in six-packs what Scaife gives in cases."

Second, the Scaife money is one important indication of an interconnection among these many organizations. Rothmyer found that "since 1973, Scaife charitable entities have given $1 million or more to each of nearly a score of organizations that are closely linked to the New Right movement." Warner noted that Scaife money has gone to 110 "ideological" organizations, including some, like the American Security Council Education Foundation, that Rothmyer did not list. Scaife does not contribute to extreme right groups like the John Birch Society; "He's not fanatical right," observes Group Research's Wes McCune. "Virtually unnoticed," Scaife has been able in Karen Rothmyer's view to "establish group after group," laying down "layer upon layer of seminars, studies, conferences, and interviews" that helped to focus interest on the issues that have become "the national agenda of debate." She documented, for example, the role of Scaife money in the 1979 Congressional debate on the SALT II treaty; at least eight critical studies were generated by Scaife-backed groups.

The professional staff members who guide the Scaife trusts and foundations have conservative connections of their own. R. Daniel McMichael, who has been with Scaife for almost twenty years, is the staff specialist in public and international affairs. McMichael is active in the Pittsburgh World Affairs Council and headed a special pre-election task force on strategic minerals for Reagan. (A November 1982 broadcast of *NOVA* by WGBH-TV in Boston, "The Cobalt Blues," questioned whether Scaife stood to gain financially from the change in U.S. policy toward South Africa.) A former employee of U.S. Steel's public-relations department, McMichael has written a novel about a Communist takeover of the United States. Richard M. Larry, a Scaife employee for approximately fifteen years, specializes in economic affairs. Larry is a Marine Corps veteran and former employee of U.S. Steel whose hobby is competitive shooting. A third member of the Scaife staff, James Shuman, has the most visible connections with the conservative network. Shuman, formerly with United Press, was an editor for *Reader's Digest.* He subsequently prepared the daily news digest in the Ford White House and then worked for the American Enterprise Institute. He also served as an aide to Panax publisher John McGoff, a partner of Scaife's.

David Warner, in his newspaper profile, suggested one more Scaife connection that should be noted—a possible involvement with the CIA. He identified Ray S. Cline, executive director of world power studies at the Georgetown CSIS and a former deputy director for intelligence in the CIA, as Scaife's main contact at the center. Scaife and McMichael were also involved, Warner asserted, in the now defunct London-based Forum World Features Ltd., the most widely circulated of the CIA news services, according to *The New York Times.* The extensive interconnections between the corporate community and the nation's intelligence effort, developed by former CIA director John McCone, have been documented by Mark Dowie and an investigative team in "The Bechtel File: How the Master Builders Protect Their Beachheads," published in *Mother Jones* (September/October 1978).

More recently, Reagan's 1980 campaign manager, William J. Casey, an OSS alumnus and conservative member of the establishment, was appointed CIA director by Reagan. Casey, a New York lawyer, headed the governing board of the relatively young conservative think tank the International Center for Economic Policy Studies—funded in part by Scaife and the Adolph Coors Foundation—when he was recruited to replace

John Sears as Reagan's campaign manager. Casey was a founding director of the conservative National Strategy Information Center in the early 1960s. Further back, he assisted with the incorporation of William Buckley's *National Review* and served as executor of the Jim Wick estate, which established the long-term funding for *Human Events*.

Besides the possible CIA connection, Scaife's involvement in Forum World Features led him to the Institute for the Study of Conflict, founded in London in 1970 by Brian Crozier, a British journalist with strong conservative views, who ran the forum. Scaife's private trusts contributed more than $1.1 million to ISC between 1973 and 1979. The ISC has published reports on threats to NATO, the infiltration of British universities by Marxists, nuclear plant construction delayed by the political left, and international terrorism. McMichael, who oversees ISC operations for Scaife, recently reported on the institute's good connections with the Thatcher government, noting also that ISC "has set up solid working relationships with the Heritage Foundation, the National Strategy Information Center, the Institute for Foreign Policy Analysis, and a number of other Scaife-supported organizations."

Scaife's involvement is relatively easy to track, since his money outlines some of the labyrinth like radioactive tracer bullets. It is more difficult to identify others of the very rich who have backed the conservative movement over the long term. David Packard, who has played a visible role in the network, is listed in a *Forbes* (September 1982) survey as the owner of a billion-dollar fortune. But the extent of his financial and other contributions to the movement cannot be determined without his voluntary disclosure.

Stephen Bechtel, Jr., plays a pivotal role in the national and international establishment. Bechtel has been described as the "reclusive" board chairman of the Bechtel Group by *The New*

York Times (December 1980) in a profile, "Bechtel and Its Links to Reagan." Two of the Bechtel Corporation's highest executives, George P. Shultz, president, and Caspar W. Weinberger, vice president and general counsel, actively supported Reagan's candidacy and had their choices of Cabinet positions. Both were former Nixon Cabinet officers. Weinberger, as Reagan's Secretary of Defense, has been involved in the massive buildup of American military forces. Schultz replaced Alexander Haig as Secretary of State in 1982. Philip Habib, a paid consultant to Bechtel since 1981, served as President Reagan's special Middle East envoy. Habib has been a senior fellow at the Hoover Institution since retiring from the State Department in 1978. The potential conflict of interest, given Bechtel's Arab clients, did not seem to concern the Washington community.

Both Stephen Bechtel, Sr., and Stephen Bechtel, Jr., have cultivated political power at the national and international levels, recruiting people like Shultz, Weinberger, and McCone. Their leadership in the Bohemian Grove, their conservative free-enterprise philosophy, and their Stanford-Hoover connections suggest a possible Bechtel interest in the long-term development of the conservative movement. Mark Dowie reports that in 1978 the elder Bechtel was one of the five richest men in the United States, with personal wealth exceeding $700 million.

The Bechtels exercise power privately at the top levels of government and the corporate world. The Bechtel Group is one of the giant privately controlled U.S. companies, ranked third by *Dun's Review* in 1978 and fifth by *Fortune* in May 1982. (A number of the corporations most frequently associated with the conservative movement and the politics of the far right are also privately held: Koch Industries, Amway, Reader's Digest Association, [Chicago] Tribune Company, Deering Milliken, and Hunt Oil, to mention only a few. "For reasons that touch at the heart of laissez-faire individualism," noted *Dun's*, "they prize their privacy above all else.")

Bechtel influence is rarely displayed publicly in the manner of the Scaife charities. The Bechtel Foundation's open contribution to Milton Friedman's *Free to Choose* TV series was unusual, although the foundation distributes an undisclosed amount of money to several conservative organizations, including the American Enterprise Institute, the Heritage Foundation, the Institute for Contemporary Studies, The Media Institute, the Pacific Institute, and the Pacific Legal Foundation.

The Smith Richardson Foundation made its mark by bankrolling an idea. Under President R. Randolph Richardson, the foundation has become "*the* source of financing in the supply-side revolution," according to the movement's chief propagandist, Jude Wanniski. "It's become the place to go if you have a project that needs money."

In 1975, Richardson asked Irving Kristol to help him recruit new staff for the Smith Richardson Foundation. Nathan Glazer, Kristol's co-editor at *The Public Interest* (funded in part by Richard Scaife), told Kristol about one of his Harvard thesis advisees, Leslie Lenkowsky. Richardson then hired Lenkowsky on Kristol's recommendation. Kristol next referred Jude Wanniski, whose early article on supply-side economics he had published in *The Public Interest* in 1975, to Lenkowsky. As a result, Smith Richardson provided a $40,000 grant for Wanniski in 1976 that led to the publication of *The Way the World Works*, the first popular book-length treatment of supply-side thought.

Chris Welles reported in *Esquire* that Wanniski and Lenkowsky convinced Richardson of the correctness of the supply-side idea. Welles also credited Wanniski with converting Kristol to the supply-side faith, as well as Robert L. Bartley, his boss at *The Wall Street Journal* editorial page, Congressman Jack Kemp, and (through his aide, Jeffrey Bell) candidate Ronald Reagan. Kemp recruited Paul Craig Roberts and Norman Ture, two "moderate" supply-siders with long-standing connections in the network, to draft and promote what became the Kemp-Roth tax-cut package. The work of Harvard's Martin Feldstein on cuts in the capital-gains tax and a few other academic studies "gave an air of respectability to the whole movement" to cut taxes, according to Randolph Penner of the American Enterprise Institute. (AEI appointed Wanniski a fellow while he was at the *Journal*.) Perhaps the most important endorsement, making supply-side seem intellectually credible, was Milton Friedman's support of the Kemp-Roth bill as a means to force a reduction in government spending.

Meanwhile, Smith Richardson made numerous grants for developing supply-side theory to groups like AEI, Heritage, Hoover, Martin Feldstein's National Bureau of Economic Research, and the Lehrman Institute. Lenkowsky helped create and fund the International Center for Economic Policy Studies, which he describes as a "supply-side think tank." He later hired writer George Gilder to direct the center's program and helped support Gilder's supply-side classic, *Wealth and Poverty*. Smith projects in 1982 included a $50,000 supply-side workshop for congressional staff members, organized by Bruce Bartlett, author of *Reaganomics: Supply Side in Action* and deputy director of the Joint Economic Committee. Besides direct support from conservative foundations like Smith Richardson, the supply-side movement received important backing from the U.S. Chamber of Commerce.

Conservative foundations have also funded a monetarist wing that has received far less attention than the supply-siders. Scaife has supported research by Milton Friedman at Hoover and

Karl Brunner at the University of Rochester. (Other Scaife grants have gone to Gordon Tullock and James Buchanan at the Center for Public Choice at Virginia Polytechnic Institute in Blacksburg. An informative account of the monetarist-libertarian wing of the new economics, including Tullock and Buchanan's Public Choice school, is Henri Lepage's *Tomorrow, Capitalism: The Economics of Economic Freedom* [1982]. Lepage, a French journalist and disciple of Milton Friedman, is a research associate at the Institute de l'Enterprise in Paris.) Brunner's most famous entrepreneurial project is the Shadow Open Market Committee, known in the financial community simply as "the Shadow," established in 1973 with Allan Meltzer, now a professor at Carnegie-Mellon. The Shadow, a panel of ten conservative economists, meets twice a year to study and critique actions of the Federal Reserve's policymaking arm, the Open Market Committee. Reagan undersecretary of the treasury Beryl Sprinkel and Council of Economic Advisers member Jerry Jordan are both alumni of the Shadow. Brunner also "wields enormous influence," according to Lindley H. Clark, Jr., of *The Wall Street Journal*, "mainly through the conferences he arranges and the academic journals he has started." These include an annual conference on monetary economics at Konstanz, West Germany; an annual conference at Interlaken on social and political problems; the Carnegie-Rochester conferences on economic affairs; the *Journal of Money, Credit, and Banking*; and the *Journal of Monetary Economics*. Brunner raises funds for his projects in both Europe and the United States.

Some sense of the scale of conservative investment in the various factions of "the new economics" is conveyed by a *Wall Street Journal* editorial on March 22, 1982, "Reaganomics Under Review." The editorial endorsed the President's program, citing a recent Heritage Foundation survey of its "resource bank economists." "These are the nearly 300 economists on the staffs of the various conservative think tanks that are part of an information exchange network Heritage operates, organizations like AEI, Hoover Institution, and the like." With these resources, AEI, for example, fielded a blue-ribbon Committee to Fight Inflation (a June 1980 domestic version of the Committee on the Present Danger), and Hoover co-sponsored a November 1981 conference on "Constraining Federal Taxing and Spending," which gave strong support to the balanced budget-tax limitation amendment sponsored by another infrastructure organization, the Friedman-backed National Tax Limitation Committee. In this case, a foundation joined forces with the think tanks to help shape national economic policy.

It must be acknowledged that the conservative foundations were not the first to invest in political change. Like so many other conservative techniques, this one was pioneered by liberals. During the 1970s, the Ford Foundation, to take only one example, funded many of the liberal public-interest law firms described in chapter 10.

But the differences far outweigh the similarities. Conservative foundations put more money into politics than their liberal counterparts and, as the discussion of the Bechtel and Scaife contributions has shown, much of it is private money, which need not be publicly accounted for. In these cases, at least, the funders seem to be more closely involved with the foundations that bear their names than is the case on the liberal side. Thus, in the 1980s, Ford could change the focus of its program, leaving many liberal and feminist organizations high and dry; Scaife is unlikely to make such a shift.

4

Political Action Groups: "We are Radicals"

THE MEDIA, Democratic Party professionals, and liberal-left activists have devoted most of their attention to the New Right and its allies on the religious right. With their social conservatism and anti-Communism and their hard-ball political campaigning, New Right political professionals like Paul Weyrich of the Committee for the Survival of a Free Congress and Coalitions for America, direct-mail specialist Richard Viguerie, Howard Phillips of The Conservative Caucus, Terry Dolan of the National Conservative Political Action Committee (NCPAC), and their protégé, the Reverend Jerry Falwell of the Moral Majority, have become "the enemy" for Democratic liberals, organized labor, blacks, the women's movement, gay activists, teachers' unions, environmentalists, and the political left in general. (Other "enemies" include Senator Jesse Helms in the Congress and former Secretary of the Interior James Watt.)

It is my contention that the liberals' focus is too limited. Their failure to place the New Right in historical context has led them to underestimate the conservative challenge. There are at least two deficiencies in much liberal analysis of the New Right. First, many liberals fail to perceive the interconnections among the New Right, the old right, and Republican Party organizations. Second, and more important, they fail to see the mutually supportive roles of the conservative political action groups, think tanks, and other sectors like the corporate community.

One case in point is Alan Crawford's *Thunder on the Right: The "New Right" and the Politics of Resentment* (1980), an inside view of conservative politics by a defector from the Viguerie organization. Crawford's book is filled with valuable information on the people who transformed the right into "an institutionalized, disciplined, well-organized, and well-financed movement of loosely knit affiliates" during the 1970s. But Crawford does not link political organizations with the conservative think tanks—despite common sources of corporate and foundation funding, interconnections through boards of directors and members of Congress, similar or overlapping public-relations strategies, and complementary policy agendas.

A fuller understanding of the New Right begins with its history. The so-called old and New Right span three or four generations of activists. The old right of William F. Buckley, Jr., and his associates dates back to the early 1950s. The Intercollegiate Studies Institute (ISI) of Bryn Mawr, Pennsylvania, began in 1952 as a conservative student organization, with Buckley as its first president. In 1955, Buckley founded the *National Review*, with William Rusher as publisher. Rusher and F. Clifton White, having cut their political teeth in the Young Republican National Federation (YRNF), became the political strategists of the ideologically distinct conservative movement that gained organizational control of the Republican Party in 1964. In September 1960, Buckley was host of a meeting of ninety-three college students at his Sharon, Connecticut, estate, resulting in a conservative manifesto, the Sharon Statement, and a new conservative organization known as Young Americans for Freedom (YAF). In 1961, Richard

Viguerie answered an ad in *National Review* for a political organizer and was hired by Rusher as YAF's executive secretary. Following the 1964 election, conservative activists regrouped under a new umbrella, the American Conservative Union, while a wave of conservative organizations like Goldwater's Free Society Association, United Republicans of America, and the Conservative Victory Fund appeared to supplement YAF and *Human Events*, the unofficial movement newspaper.

By the mid-1970s, with the entry of Weyrich, Coors, and Scaife, and the help of the Federal Election Campaign Act of 1974—which provided a new opportunity for Viguerie's direct-mail fund-raising—the leading New Right organizations had appeared. An example of the interaction of generations of conservative activists is Representative Robert Bauman's resignation as chairman of the American Conservative Union. When Bauman was revealed to be a homosexual in 1980, New Right leaders like Paul Weyrich called for his resignation on the grounds that he could "no longer be a credible spokesman for causes." But it was not until William F. Buckley, Jr., and other senior conservatives intervened that Bauman resigned his position.

The difference of emphasis between old and New Right should not be exaggerated. Many of the important players have remained the same since the 1950s. Phyllis Schlafly illustrates the point. Her tract, *A Choice, Not an Echo*, was one of the bibles of the Draft Goldwater movement; her conservative women's organization, the Eagle Forum, is a product of conservative consolidation and development after Goldwater; and her anti-ERA campaign was a significant victory for New Right political strategy in the 1970s and 1980s. The powerful and shadowy YRNF "syndicate" organization that trained and advanced the careers of future party leaders and professionals like the late John Ashbrook, William Brock, Donald "Buz"

Lukens, and William Timmons is another example of the continuity of personnel from the Old Right to the New.

Besides the interlocking of organizations and generations of leadership, the conservatives have excelled in developing such devices as the weekend strategy planning session (usually held at an airport motel) and the regularly scheduled coordinating meeting. The former was brought to perfection by F. Clifton White and the Goldwater organizers. A more recent example was the May 1979 Dulles Marriott strategy session for 100 conservative political, religious, and business leaders chaired by Terry Dolan, head of NCPAC. The letter of invitation, signed by eight New Right senators, outlined a set of specific guidelines to ensure that the meeting would remain "very private and confidential." More visible coordinating groups have been an organizational specialty of Paul Weyrich. The Kingston group, which has been functioning for about ten years, has over fifty participants who meet on Fridays to discuss economic and institutional issues. The Library Court group, chaired by Weyrich associate Connaught ("Connie") Marshner, meets every other Thursday to discuss New Right social issues. (The group tried recently to resolve a conservative split on antiabortion tactics.) A third Weyrich outfit, known as the Stanton group, meets on alternate Thursdays to review defense issues. The Reagan White House and New Right senators like Jesse Helms regularly send representatives to these meetings. Helms's then aide John Carbaugh has organized an even more select foreign-policy circle known as the Madison group. Membership in this Friday luncheon club is limited to conservative congressional staff aides with security clearances of top secret or higher. Yet another coordinating group on election strategy, chaired by New Right activist Morton Blackwell, meets for lunch every other Monday at the Key Bridge Marriott Hotel across the river from Washington, D.C.

The conservatives have developed what might be described as a "cadre system" for advancing the careers of people they favor. Something approximating an internal personnel promotion system was already evident by the late 1960s; it has featured prominently in Reagan Administration appointments. Senior conservatives and neoconservatives like Rusher, Viguerie, and Irving Kristol function as talent scouts, steering promising young conservatives to fellowship opportunities, research grants, publishers, or staff positions. One of the most interesting yet relatively unknown talent-spotting agencies is the ISI-Weaver Fellow network. Over the past twenty years, Weaver Fellowships have financed advanced studies for close to 300 conservative university graduates.

Among the most successful Weaver alumni is Heritage Foundation President Edwin Feulner. Feulner is a 1965 Weaver Fellow and a trustee of ISI who has held a range of positions within the network: administrative assistant to Congressman Philip M. Crane (R-Illinois), confidential aide to Defense Secretary Melvin R. Laird, executive director of the Republican Study Committee, and fellow at both the Hoover Institution and the Georgetown Center. Feulner appointed former Reagan National Security Adviser Richard V. Allen—also an ISI trustee active in the ISI and conservative networks since his undergraduate years at Notre Dame in the mid-1950s— a Heritage Foundation Distinguished Fellow. Reagan's Secretary of the Navy, John F. Lehman, an outspoken defender when Allen was under attack, is a 1964 Weaver Fellow with a string of top appointments in Republican Administrations. Charles Heatherly, who edited Heritage's *Mandate for Leadership* and is now executive secretary to Reagan's Secretary of Education, is a former ISI regional director. Wayne H. Valis, Reagan special assistant for public liaison with the American business community, once edited ISI's *Intercollegiate*

Review (one of five journals published by the organization) and has been active in ISI since 1963. Paul Craig Roberts, who served on the staff of *The Wall Street Journal* editorial page and as a senior fellow in political economy at the Georgetown CSIS before being appointed Reagan's Assistant Secretary of the Treasury for Economic Policy, has been a faculty member of ISI's summer institutes. Roberts, a leading publicist for supply-side economics, left the administration in January 1982 to become the first occupant of the William E. Simon Chair in Political Economy at CSIS, endowed with $2 million in pledges from twenty corporate and foundation donors such as W. R. Grace and Company.

Left-liberal researchers, using the files of Group Research, Inc., of Washington, D.C., the major research organization that has monitored the right, have partly documented the extensive interlocking directorates and interconnections among the conservative political action groups. Richard Viguerie has been especially adept in training a political cadre and establishing, staffing, and funding new organizations. A similar network operates in the YAF.

Conservative groups and their leaders also span the spectrum from "responsible" right-of-center organizations like The Conservative Caucus to far right groups like the Liberty Lobby, an anti-Zionist organization, and the John Birch Society. Two points about the conservative spectrum should be stressed. First, groups closer to the center have always been able to work with groups on the far right. Goldwater's "extremism in the defense of liberty" speech in 1964 signaled an effective working alliance in the elections. Although the extreme right has been less vocal and less visible in the media since the 1960s, it has maintained its organizational strength and adapted to new political technologies. The New Right–Birch connections have been most visible in the Schlafly organization, although they are also important in the religious right. One Reagan nominee (Warren Richardson, as Assistant Secretary of Health and Human Services) withdrew from consideration when it was revealed that he had been general counsel of the far right Liberty Lobby from 1969 to 1973.

Second, and perhaps more significant, some organizations have made an effort to gain public respectability and shed their ultra-right images. The Hoover Institution, for example, shifted its emphasis from cold war anti-Communism to American studies and public policy over the 1970s. Georgetown CSIS followed a similar course. The National Right to Work Committee (following the lead of Mobil Oil) has placed advertisements for its legal defense fund in *The New York Review of Books*. The Heritage Foundation alliance with neoconservatives has already been noted.

The most dramatic example of this effort to "clean up" the far right is the case of the American Security Council (ASC). Founded in Chicago in 1955 as the Mid-American Research Library, the organization's initial function was to compile files on suspected Communists who might apply for jobs in the private sector. Sponsoring corporations included Sears, Roebuck and Company, Motorola Incorporated, and Marshall Field and Company. At its peak, the council served more than 1,500 firms as the private equivalent of the FBI or Senate Internal Security Committee, with 6 million personnel file cards and a specialized subversive-activities library. In 1966, the Chicago library was closed and the American Security Council moved to the Blue Ridge foothills in Boston, Virginia. President John Fisher, who came to the organization from Sears in 1956, announced that the council was shifting its focus to "international security and nuclear strategy." Fisher is another figure in the labyrinth whose involvement spans more than two decades. (The files, which have been described by some observers as "America's largest private file on the political beliefs of individuals," are currently part of the council's Sol Feinstone Library for the Survival of Freedom.)

With a staff of thirty and annual mailings in the millions, ASC had approximately 30,000 members in 1983. During the nuclear-freeze initiative campaign, it provided coordination and limited funding to local opposition groups. In the fall of 1978, ASC received national television news coverage as the host for the then prime minister of Rhodesia, Ian Smith. Fisher also recruited former *Newsweek* foreign editor Philip C. Clarke as his press liaison. ASC has been the organizational force behind such conservative initiatives as the Coalition for Peace through Strength.

The conservative political action groups have made full use of the latest political technology, copying earlier liberal successes, like the National Committee for an Effective Congress and Common Cause. (California Common Cause executive director Walter Zelman acknowledges that his organization has deemphasized many of its original lobbying techniques because they had been so effectively eclipsed by conservative and business lobbies.) In direct mail, the conservatives, as well as the Republican Party organization, have been pioneers.

The Viguerie Company (known as TVC) is a major nexus for conservative organizational activity via direct mail. Starting with the names of 12,500 contributors to the 1964 Goldwater campaign, Viguerie has systematically built a computer data bank containing some 20 million names and 4.5 million contributors. Some of TVC's past and present clients include: NCPAC, The Conservative Caucus, Christian Crusade, Korean Cultural Freedom Foundation (Reverend Sun Myung Moon), Pink Sheet on the Left, National Right to Work Committee, Gun Owners of America, Young Americans for Freedom, Committee for the Survival of a Free Congress, and numerous election campaigns such as those of the late Georgia Democratic representative Larry McDonald (who succeeded Robert Welch as head of the John Birch Society) and Senator Jesse Helms. TVC also worked on several of its clients' special projects, including Radio Free Asia, Panama Canal Truth Squad, and Americans Against Union Control of Government.

Largely as a result of Viguerie's expertise, New Right political action committees (PACs) led the field of political fund-raising groups monitored by the Federal Election Commission in 1980. Six of the ten largest, and the top three, PACs were New Right groups. The largest PAC in the country was Senator Helms's National Congressional Club (started, according to some reports, with aid from TVC but now an integral part of Helms's political empire), which raised $7.9 million in the 1979–80 reporting period and made $4.6 million in "independent expenditures" in support of the Reagan presidential campaign. A close second was Terry Dolan's National Conservative Political Action Committee (NCPAC), a TVC client, with $7.6 million raised and $3.3 million in independent expenditures, mostly targeted at liberal Democratic senators. Total Viguerie fund-raising in 1980 was estimated by sources close to the company at between $35 million and $40 million.

At least as important as the actual funds raised is the investment in developing and updating mailing lists both for TVC and for its clients. The conservatives have skillfully built an independent communications tool capable of reaching targeted single-issue constituencies. When Howard Phillips, national director of The Conservative Caucus, boasts that "we organize discontent" and "must prove our ability to get revenge on people who go against us," he and his organization have at their disposal a resource that is at least a decade (by Viguerie's estimate) ahead of anything the liberals have.

TVC publishes a glossy, full-color magazine, *Conserva-*

tive Digest, founded in 1975 and operated at a substantial annual deficit by some reports. Alan Crawford, the magazine's first assistant editor, says that it was aimed at the George Wallace constituency as well as traditional conservatives, and that its editors' library included Birch periodicals but not more moderate conservative publications like *Human Events*. (Crawford left when it became clear that *Conservative Digest* was "little more than an adjunct of the Viguerie fund-raising operation, functioning to promote 'rising stars on the right' [many of whom were TVC clients] as well as to cover political developments.") Viguerie also published *The New Right Report*, a twice-monthly newsletter for political activists until 1983.

TVC has trained scores of young conservatives in direct mail, communications, and other organizational skills, feeding them into staff positions in the Republican Party, Congress, and various conservative organizations. Of the fifty major political direct-mail consultants, about forty are conservative Republican. Stephen Winchell and Associates, a conservative Republican firm formed in 1976, has contracts with the three Republican national campaign committees. Winchell is a former executive vice president of the Viguerie Company. Former Viguerie aide Morton Blackwell, who organized the Committee for Responsible Youth Politics and is now special assistant to the President in the Reagan White House, has played a central role in developing young conservative talent. Viguerie has occasionally considered expanding the size and scope of his 300-member firm's operations. One of his most ambitious efforts was the founding of a conservative Council for National Policy to rival the Council on Foreign Relations. The council includes most of the activist leadership on the right as well as conservative contributors like Joseph Coors and William Herbert and Nelson Bunker Hunt.

Another example of the advanced organizational skill of the

conservatives is afforded by Paul Weyrich, considered by many to be the organizational genius of the New Right. One of the most impressive Weyrich creations, relatively unknown to the media and general public, is the Free Congress Research and Education Foundation, Inc., a tax-exempt affiliate of the Weyrich PAC, the Committee for the Survival of a Free Congress. Since 1978 the Free Congress Foundation has published a weekly newsletter, *The Political Report*, which features the best reporting on congressional districts and candidates (including field interviews) that many Washington professionals have ever seen. In 1980 the foundation started another monthly newsletter, *Initiative and Referendum Report*, to provide comprehensive, up-to-date information about important state and local issues. A coalition project involving national and regional conferences studied coalition formation in legislatures as "an important political trend" of the 1980s. The foundation also sponsors post-election analysis conferences for campaign managers and political consultants. Such research complements the work of the network and its coordinating strategy groups. For example, the foundation sponsored a study on "Negative Campaigns and Negative Votes: The 1980 Elections" by pollster V. Lance Tarrance, Jr., assessing the impact of groups like NCPAC and the Moral Majority on three Senate races. A third newsletter, the monthly *Family Protection Report*, edited by Connie Marshner, covers Washington, state, and local developments "of importance to the traditional family and its values."

The steady development of numerous conservative political action groups, and the growth of the conservative think tanks, represents something quite new—in available resources and sophistication—in American politics. Add to this the ideological fervor of the conservative activists and there is a formidable force for change. The strident anti-Communism of the Sharon statement ("The forces of International Communism are, at present, the greatest single threat to those liberties" and "The United States should stress victory over, rather than coexistence with, this menace") survives in conservative/neoconservative pressures on Reagan to terminate the West European-Soviet gas pipeline, intervene militarily in Central America, and in the 1983 Miami speech in which Reagan called the Soviet Union the focus of all evil in the world. On economic and social policy issues, younger conservatives are equally determined. "We are different from previous generations of conservatives," says Paul Weyrich. "We are no longer working to preserve the status quo. We are radicals, working to overturn the present power structure of this country."

5

The Religious Right:
The Electronic Ministers

PERHAPS NO DEVELOPMENT in the conservative labyrinth has received more public attention than the emergence of the religious right as a major political force in 1979–80. Wes McCune of Group Research, who has monitored the right for two decades, calls it "the most important development on the right since 1964." But the deeper significance of the religious right has frequently been underestimated.

The new political strength of the religious right derives from two separate developments, the rise of evangelical Christianity as an alternative culture in America, complete with an independent communications network; and the active cultivation of this and other religious communities by the political conservatives. Under the leadership of the New Right, an alliance of mutual convenience has been established between an important part of the conservative religious community and the conservative political coalition.

Three books published in the past few years provide extensive commentary on the Christian evangelical movement. They include Jeremy Rifkin and Ted Howard, *The Emerging Order: God in an Age of Scarcity* (1979); Flo Conway and Jim Siegelman, *Holy Terror: The Fundamentalist War on America's Freedoms in Religion, Politics and Our Private Lives* (1982);

and Perry Deane Young, *God's Bullies: Native Reflections on Preachers and Politics* (1982). These observers estimate that there are 45 million evangelical Christians in the United States. Nearly one in every three Americans now claims to have been "born again." (The literature of the Christian right cites a goal of 50 million. The issue of Viguerie's *Conservative Digest* [August 1979] devoted to "Mobilizing the Moral Majority" estimated that "these may be nearly 100 million Americans— 50 million born-again Protestants, 30 million morally conservative Catholics, 3 million Mormons, and 2 million Orthodox Jews—from which to draw members of a pro-family, Bible-believing coalition.") While polls underscore the diversity of political opinion among born-again Christians, New Right conservatives have retained pollsters like Lance Tarrance and Associates of Houston to help them target their appeals.

The evangelical Christian communications system now rivals the major commercially sponsored networks. More than 1,300 radio stations (1 out of every 7 in America) are Christian-owned and operated. Two Christian TV networks, using satellites, reach 35 Christian TV stations and TV affiliates in all major United States markets, with an estimated audience of almost 40 million. The PTL (People That Love, formerly Praise The Lord) television network had 179 TV affiliates in 1981, compared with 204 for ABC. In that year, contributions of $25 million to PTL supported a Charlotte, North Carolina, broadcast center equipped with nearly $2 million worth of the most advanced communications technology and a staff of over 550 employees. PTL, started in the mid-1970s, is already the fourth-largest purchaser of air time in the United States. A second Christian Broadcast Network (CBN) also operates a worldwide satellite communications system from Virginia Beach, Virginia, with a staff of 700 and a $22 million operating budget as of 1981. Both PTL and CBN built multimillion-dollar communications schools and CBN plans a network news show to compete with ABC, CBS, and NBC.

In addition, Jerry Falwell, Billy Graham, Rex Humbard, Oral Roberts, and Robert Schuller each have multimillion-dollar TV and radio operations. Falwell's radio show, *The Old Time Gospel Hour*, aired on 300 radio stations in 1982; Sunday worship services from his Thomas Road Baptist Church were broadcast on 373 television stations. Yet the size of the weekly audiences of these preachers is in dispute. Estimates have ranged from 7–10 million to as high as 115–130 million. The combined income of the "electronic church" may reach nearly $500 million per year, the *National Journal* reported.

The links between the conservative network and the evangelical community are provided by the so-called electronic ministers, fundamentalist preachers organized by Falwell, who took an active role in the 1980 elections. "This effort to build a single-minded new electoral bloc," concluded Dudley Clendinen of *The New York Times*, "is being led by a national network of men who have known each other years in the insular church community." Some key figures in Falwell's personal network are the premier TV evangelist, James Robison of Fort Worth, Texas, who was host of the hour-long TV program "Wake Up America: We're All Hostages!" in June 1980, featuring Governor John Connally; Representative Philip M. Crane; General Lewis Walt; Pat Robertson, son of former U.S. senator A. William Robertson (D–Virginia), who heads CBN and its daily anchor program, the *700 Club*; and Dr. Bill Bright, founder and president of Campus Crusade for Christ International. The internationally syndicated *700 Club*, according to Flo Conway and Jim Siegelman, in *Holy Terror*, "may be as blatantly political as any program on television." Robertson (whom they consider the media "wiz" of the evangelical movement) and black co-host Ben Kinchlow regularly present features on domestic and international topics. The Christian message is muted.

Connections between the far right and fundamentalist Christianity are not new. They were evident during the Draft Goldwater years in Reverend Billy James Hargis's Christian Crusade and Dr. Fred Schwarz's Christian Anti-Communism Crusade. H. L. Hunt and J. Howard Pew (Sun Oil) were among the wealthy Birch supporters who funded the early Christian right. Richard Viguerie was indelibly impressed by Schwarz's *You Can Trust the Communists—To Be Communists*. Former Schwarz aide Gilburn Durand, also a recruiter for the Birch Society and the Draft Goldwater movement, who purchased 300,000 copies of Phyllis Schlafly's *A Choice, Not an Echo*, turned up in 1974 organizing Catholic clergy in "Operation Avalanche," "designed to mobilize the 43 million Catholics into an army of pro-life political activists."

An indication of the amount of money conservative Christians are investing in their infrastructure is the Crusade for Christ. A consortium of conservative business leaders led by Nelson Bunker Hunt, one of the heirs of the Hunt Oil Company fortune, and Wallace Johnson, founder of Holiday Inns, is working with Bill Bright to evangelize every man, woman, and child on earth in preparation for the second coming of Christ. Over $30 million has been raised, including at least $15.5 million from Hunt. Hunt, whose Birch Society background is documented by Conway and Siegelman in *Holy Terror*, also made a contribution of $1 million to the Moral Majority in 1981, according to Perry Deane Young.

A major transition in the religious right occurred in 1975. Richard M. DeVos, the president of Amway Corporation and, from early 1981 until mid-1982, finance chairman of the Republican National Committee, and a group of conservative businessmen including John Talcott of Ocean Spray Cranberries and Art De Moss, board chairman of the National Liberty Insurance Corporation, took control of the tax-exempt Christian Freedom Foundation. (J. Howard Pew started the foundation in 1950 with a grant of $50,000. During the 1960s, the various Pew trusts contributed more than $2 million to CFF. In 1974, the Pew Freedom Trust contributed $300,000. DeVos, who, according to Thomas B. Mechling, has functioned for years as "the quiet Godfather and financial angel of the Religious Right Movement," contributed $25,000 to CFF in 1974.) Their purpose, apparently, was to use the foundation's tax-exempt status to further religious right organizing efforts and to channel funds into Third Century Publishers. Third Century puts out *One Nation Under God*, which provides a political rationale for the religious right, and *In the Spirit of '76*, a handbook for winning elections. Art De Moss admitted publicly that the purpose of CFF was to elect Christian conservatives to Congress in 1976: "The vision is to rebuild the foundations of the Republic as it was when first founded—a 'Christian Republic.' We must return to the faith of our fathers."

DeVos's involvement in the religious right may help to explain why defense of the free-enterprise system is so high on its agenda. The Moral Majority's stated goal, for example, is "to defend the free enterprise system, the family, and Bible morality." Jay Van Andel, chairman of Amway, and DeVos have used their corporation and their personal connections to sell free enterprise in a big way. Amway's public-affairs activities include the Institute for Free Enterprise, which has sponsored education workshops for 2,000 teachers; a nationwide newspaper advertising campaign rivaling that of Mobil Oil and attacking inflation, government deficits, government regulation, and high taxes; a monthly column under the byline of Van Andel and DeVos distributed free to 1,500 small daily and weekly newspapers; and donations to conservative groups ranging from the Heritage Foundation to the American Economic Foundation. DeVos insists that he is a traditional rather than an ultraconservative Republican. His extensive contributions to religious broadcasting (Amway foundations contributed $600,000 in 1979, while DeVos and his wife contributed at least another $118,000) usually go to evangelicals like Robert Schuller, who have steered away from controversial political topics.

Ed McAteer, a fundamentalist active in a wide range of Christian organizations and employed at the time as Southern sales marketing manager for Colgate Palmolive, joined the staff of CFF in 1976. About a year later, McAteer had impressed Howard Phillips enough to be named national field director of Phillips's New Right grass-roots organization, The Conservative Caucus. Phillips introduced McAteer to Viguerie and Weyrich, and in turn McAteer introduced Phillips to Jerry Falwell and Pat Robertson. Historians of the New Right date the Moral Majority to that connection. (A remarkable television portrait of McAteer, entitled "Portrait of an American Zealot" was included in Barbara Jordan's PBS documentary series, *Crisis to Crisis*, on July 30, 1982.) McAteer's network led in 1979 to the formation of the Religious Roundtable, the major public coordinating organization of the New Right-religious right, which he heads. At about the same time, Paul Weyrich befriended Reverend Robert J. Billings, who had made an unsuccessful bid for Congress in Indiana in 1976. Weyrich persuaded Billings to return to Washington and begin a Christian lobbying group for Christian schools. Billings currently serves as a contact for the religious right on the Reagan Department of Education, where he is director of the Regional Liaison Unit.

By 1980, four new organizations had been created: Christian

Right; the Moral Majority, ecumenical in emphasis, with Billings as executive director; McAteer's Religious Roundtable; and Washington for Jesus (now America for Jesus), which mobilized 200,000 conservative Christians for an April 1980 Washington rally and subsequent state rallies.

The alliance between the New Right and the religious right has yielded substantial benefits to both sides. McAteer has been working hard, "telling these people [his religious network] . . . who Paul Weyrich is, who Richard Viguerie is, who Howard Phillips is. See, I knew that those fellows had the information that our people needed." Between August 22 and November 2, 1980, McAteer's Roundtable organized educational and training meetings for some 40,000 pastors, staffed in part by the Weyrich and Phillips organizations. Weyrich was a central organizer of the Roundtable's 1980 political action seminar and rally in Dallas, which drew 18,000. Speakers included candidate Ronald Reagan (who used the occasion to plug "creation science," the fundamentalist answer to evolution), New Right senators Jesse Helms of North Carolina and William Armstrong of Colorado, former Texas governor John B. Connally, Phyllis Schlafly, and Falwell, Robison, and Robertson. Weyrich in turn appreciates the resources the fundamentalists bring to the coalition: "They have mastered the use of television and radio for their efforts, and this will make communications easier." Weyrich and his associate Connie Marshner have been guests on Robertson's *700 Club*, as well as Reverend James Baker's *Praise the Lord*. "We've been at meetings," Weyrich comments, "where perfect strangers have come up and said, 'Oh, I saw you on the *700 Club*, and if Pat says you're great—you're great.'"

The interchange of skills and resources runs much deeper than even these examples suggest. The New Right has trained or provided personnel for groups like Christian Voice. This is particularly evident in the Right-to-Life movement, an important stream within the religious right. One pro-life PAC, Life-PAC, is run out of the Washington office of Lee Edwards, a YAF alumnus from the early 1960s (and former editor of YAF's *New Guard*). Another national PAC, Stop the Baby-killers, is chaired by former YRNF head and former Ohio representative Donald (Buz) Lukens, who is currently on the Board of Directors of the American Legislative Exchange Council (ALEC). Peter Gemma, executive director of the National Pro-Life Political Action Committee (NPLPAC), was national director and a former political consultant to Representative Philip Crane of Illinois. NPLPAC sponsored the first national pro-life political action conference in Chicago in May 1979. The New Right has also provided groups like Christian Voice with ready-made congressional advisory committees that provide instant access to New Right senators and representatives and their staffs. The Viguerie organization has given religious right political action committees a direct-mail capability. ALEC furnishes a network to conservative state legislators. Of particular note are ALEC model bills like the Textbook Content Standards Act, now being introduced in state legislatures with the support of the religious right. The Heritage Foundation has prepared background research on "secular humanism" (Heritage staffer Onalee McGraw is an authority on the subject), the latest target of the religious right. Timothy LaHaye, author of *The Battle for the Family* and the leading New Right preacher against secular humanism, is president of the Viguerie-sponsored Council for National Policy.

The religious right carries more than its own weight in the alliance. Falwell's Moral Majority, like the think tanks, generates issues for conservatives. The Moral Majority's "Top-

Secret Battle Plan for 1982," distributed to members, outlined a campaign against homosexual influence in television and in state and municipal government; a strategy for passage of a Human Life statute and/or Human Life Amendment; a strategy to counter the influence of the American Civil Liberties Union (including a new Legal Defense Foundation with a computer-accessed law library); a National Conference on Pornography for district attorneys, prosecutors, sheriffs, and police chiefs; an anti-ERA strategy coordinated with Phyllis Schlafly and her Eagle Forum; and a major push for the Family Protection Act. The Moral Majority has also been the major supporter of the Coalition for Better Television (CBT), chaired by Reverend Donald E. Wildmon of Tupelo, Mississippi. In spring 1981, CBT, which claims to speak for 1,800 organizations, threatened to boycott all TV shows it found objectionable. A few major corporate advertisers, such as Procter and Gamble and Smith Kline, agreed to review their sponsorship of programs. When the networks also agreed to review their programming, Wildmon called off the boycott. However, in March 1982, CBT determined that the networks were backsliding, and singled out NBC and its parent company, RCA, for a new boycott on the grounds that NBC "discriminates against Christian values."

Christian Voice distributes TV and radio tapes by such New Right figures as Senator Helms and former California representative Robert Dornan to the "electronic church." TV ads to stimulate support for Christian Voice have been aired on Praise The Lord. The National Christian Action Coalition, headed by William Billings, released a 29-minute color film for the 1980 elections, "Politics: A Christian Viewpoint," featuring Weyrich, Helms, Senator Gordon Humphrey, the late Representative Larry McDonald, and Representative Bill Dannemeyer. The National Christian Action Coalition and Christian

Voice also pioneered "morality ratings" for evaluating legislative incumbents in the 1980 races.

Some observers believe that the new religious activists are the infantry for the political right. McAteer points out that there are 300,000 pastors in this country with an average church membership between 600 and 700. One pastor "who is prepared to articulate the positions properly" can reach a large audience. After a 1980 national survey, Haynes Johnson of *The Washington Post* concluded that Falwell's followers "have great organization, commitment, desire, hunger, and the absolutely unshakable faith that they are correct. And they want to impose it on the majority." Building on the fundamentalist Bible Belt that was the foundation of the 1964 Goldwater "Southern strategy," Falwell and the electronic ministers have created a national constituency that meshes with the new conservative politics of the 1980s.

It is important to note that both the New Right and the religious right have extensive staff connections within the Reagan White House. Terry Dolan's brother, Anthony, is chief speech writer for the President, and his sister, Maiselle, is also on the White House staff. Reagan has named one of the most effective New Right activists, former Viguerie associate Morton Blackwell, as White House religious affairs adviser, an important position for building connections with the religious right.

In Pat Robertson's view, the new religious coalition has enough votes to run the country. "And when the people say, 'We've had enough,' we are going to take over." Gary Potter, president of the Catholics for Christian Political Action, elaborates this threat: "When the Christian majority takes over this country, there will be no satanic churches, no more free distribution of pornography, no more abortion on demand, and no more talk of rights for homosexuals. After the Christian majority takes control, pluralism will be seen as immoral and evil and the state will not permit anybody the right to practice evil." Falwell sets a more modest goal: "I think we should be the moral conscience of a nation."

The evangelical community as a whole does not endorse the Falwell-Robertson political line. Although the religious right effectively dominates the National Religious Broadcasters, members of the parent National Association of Evangelicals have objected to what they see as an effort to form a Christian party identifying particular political and ethical positions with a biblical viewpoint. The Reverend Billy Graham remarks that just as liberals organized in the sixties, so "conservatives certainly have a right to organize in the eighties, but it would disturb me if there was a wedding between the religious fundamentalists and the political right. The hard right has no interest in religion except to manipulate it." But Graham, at sixty-seven, is of a different generation. The Billy Graham Evangelistic Association's budget is half of fifty-one-year-old Jerry Falwell's.

The New Right–religious right coalition has been telegraphing its major political punch for some time—a joint strategy for passage of the Family Protection Act (FPA). Weyrich has predicted that "the family will be to the decade of the 1980s what environmentalism and consumerism have been to the 1970s and what the Vietnam War was to the 1960s. . . . What the right-to-life movement has managed to put together on the abortion issue is only a sample of what is to come when the full range of family and educational issues becomes the focus of debate in the 1980s." Falwell's Moral Majority intends "to create the largest coalition in support of the [Family Protection] Act ever formed by conservatives in the history of America." The drafting of redundant provisions in the FPA, as well as in the parallel ALEC model statutes for state legislatures, facilitates the forming of alliances with a broad range of groups in support of the legislation.

The coalition's agenda, however, is by no means limited to social conservatism. Falwell and his fellow electronic ministers have been flying to Taiwan and Israel in search of international connections, the most famous of which has been Falwell's alliance with Begin. The religious right also opposed the SALT II treaty and supported Ian Smith's regime in Rhodesia. The extension of the religious right into foreign and national security policy has generated working relationships with groups like the American Security Council and Jesse Helms's "shadow State Department." The ASC role in the Religious Roundtable has gone unnoticed. ASC president John Fisher, along with Helms, is one of the political members of the Roundtable's "Council of 56" (the number of signers of the Declaration of Independence), which, according to *The New York Times*, comprises "virtually all the leaders of the New Right, from the Congress, the electronic ministers, the tactical and issue organizations, and the independent church networks." The Roundtable's executive director, Bill Skelton, who handles day-to-day operations under McAteer, is a fundamentalist who served as president of the Christian Freedom Foundation for ten years, as well as administrative director of the American Security Council.

The growing sophistication of the Christian right poses problems for political liberals. Contrasting the 1960s and the 1980s, labor leader and civil-rights activist James Farmer observed: "The right-wing agenda is being hidden by religious language and additional followers are being mobilized by emotional appeals to God and Jesus. The agenda has become more difficult to expose and confront because it is now indirect and cloaked in emotionalism." While Falwell's Liberty

Baptist College still advertises in Birch and Liberty Lobby publications, connections with the far right have been played down. The Christian anti-Communism of an earlier era has been replaced by a denunciation of "secular humanism" and an emphasis on moral issues.

John Connally courted the religious right during 1979 and 1980. Widely regarded as the presidential choice of corporate America, he recruited Richard Viguerie to his campaign after Philip Crane's Viguerie-backed presidential campaign ground to a halt. Connally met with Falwell and a group of religious right ministers at his Texas ranch in the summer of 1979, delivered a major address at fundamentalist Bob Jones University in Greenville, South Carolina, and agreed to participate in Robison's TV special, "Wake Up America." While Falwell found that Connally, in contrast to Reagan, did not have a clear understanding of some of the moral issues his group felt deeply about, he concluded, "It won't take a great deal for me to get excited about Connally, because he is a leader." The Burlington, Massachusetts, computer firm that services Jerry Falwell's master list, as well as those of many other evangelicals, Epsilon Data Management, also managed Connally's computer lists during the campaign.

Although the corporate (Connally)–New Right (Viguerie)–Christian right (Falwell) alliance did not survive the Republican primaries, it may foreshadow a future alignment in American politics.

6

The Corporations:
Making Our Voices Heard

As IMPRESSIVE as the resources of Jerry Falwell and the electronic ministers may be, they are dwarfed by those of corporate America. Belief in free enterprise as a secular faith is probably an even more powerful force in American culture than religious fundamentalism. The corporate sector is an important part of the story of the conservative labyrinth and its development. Since the early 1970s, the business community has organized itself to assume a far more direct and aggressive role in American politics, often in alliance with the conservatives.

As early as the 1940s and 1950s, some corporations and executives actively supported conservative organizations and causes. Lewis H. Brown, the president of Johns Manville Corporation, founded the American Enterprise Association, the predecessor of AEI, in 1943. It operated on an annual budget of about $80,000 in its early years. In 1954, William J. Baroody was recruited from the U.S. Chamber of Commerce to become AEA's executive vice president. (Baroody was a Chamber of Congress official from 1950 to 1953 and associate editor of *American Economic Security*.) We have already noted the role of Sears, Roebuck and other corporations in the founding of the American Security Council in 1955. The Buckley family's oil fortune and a small number of corporate advertisers kept the *National Review* solvent during its early years. The National Right to Work Committee (NRTWC), the leading anti-union organization in the labyrinth, was organized in 1955 by former representative Fred Hartley, co-sponsor of the Taft-Hartley Act, and Edwin S. Dillard, a Virginia box manufacturer and early supporter of the John Birch Society. (Reed Larson, who has headed the NRTWC and NRTWC Foundation since 1959, is another important conservative whose career spans two decades. Larson has consistently refused to reveal information about corporate backers of his organizations, successfully resisting a request from federal judge Charles R. Richey in Washington.)

Lemuel R. Boulware of the General Electric Corporation hired Ronald Reagan in 1955 to tour the company's 135 plants, presenting conservative management views. Publicist Edward Langley, who has written on Reagan's GE years, remarks that GE was "a company so obsessed with conservatism that it was not unlike the John Birch Society. . . . There was never anything like the Boulware years in other industries." (Reagan was dropped by GE by 1963 as his political career became more public, although Boulware remained a patron until at least 1976, when they parted company over Reagan's choice of Richard Schweiker as his running mate.)

A new phase in corporate support of the conservatives began in the mid-1960s, following the Goldwater presidential campaign. Baroody took a "leave of absence" from AEI to organize a brain trust that included AEI affiliates like economist Milton Friedman, national security expert Warren Nutter, and Baroody's former AEI aide, Glenn Campbell, at Hoover. Denison Kitchell from the Goldwater campaign served as the chief contact with the Baroody group. After surviving an intensive two-year IRS examination of its tax-exempt status, AEI broadened its appeal to the corporate community, emphasizing a more centrist, although still pro-business, policy stance. David

Packard, co-founder of Hewlett-Packard, and Republican representative Melvin R. Laird addressed groups of potential corporate sponsors on behalf of AEI, Hoover, and Georgetown CSIS. (Richard M. Nixon appointed Laird Secretary of Defense in his first administration; Laird chose Packard as his undersecretary. Laird is currently senior counselor of the Reader's Digest Association, a privately held corporation allied with the conservatives. Packard returned to Hewlett-Packard.) Baroody recruited top corporate executives to the AEI Board of Trustees, including J. Schmidt, vice chairman of the board of Mobil Oil, who headed the AEI board for a number of years, as well as executives from Procter and Gamble, Standard Oil of Indiana, Standard Oil of California, General Electric, and Rockwell International.

By the 1970s, other conservatives were making even more sophisticated appeals to the corporate community. Irving Kristol, a senior fellow at AEI and author of *Two Cheers for Capitalism*, encourages a more deliberate strategy on the part of business people concerned about the direction of political change. "He's put spine into the business community," comments Kristol's AEI colleague Ben Wattenberg. Another advocate of a new political hard line in the corporate world is William E. Simon, whose conservative manifesto, *A Time for Truth*, was funded and published by the Reader's Digest Press. "Funds generated by business (by which I mean profits, funds in business foundations and contributions from individual businessmen) must rush by multimillions to the aid of liberty . . . to funnel desperately needed funds to scholars, social scientists, writers, and journalists who understand the relationship between political and economic liberty," Simon urged. Besides grants "in exchange for books, books, and more books," he called on business to "cease the mindless subsidizing of colleges and universities whose departments of economics, government, politics, and history are hostile to capitalism" and to divert funds from "the media which serve as megaphones for anticapitalist opinion" to those that are more "pro-freedom" and "pro-business." (One interesting response to Simon's appeal is worth mentioning. In 1979, *Argosy*, a popular men's magazine of the outdoors, published since 1882, became pro-business and conservative, with articles on the tax revolt, government regulation, bureaucracy, and budget deficits.)

Corporate participation in conservative political action has been much less obvious than its support of conservative think tanks. It should be noted, however, that executives of some large corporations work closely with the political side of the network. Among those attending the "private" New Right strategy conference at the Dulles Marriott in May 1979 were a vice president of Chase Manhattan, an executive vice president of Adolph Coors Brewery, a group vice president of public affairs for Dart Industries, a vice president for government affairs of Georgia Pacific Corporation, and the director of government affairs for the National Association of Manufacturers, not to mention representatives of several smaller corporations.

While the corporate sector provides personnel, funding, and a range of services to conservatives, the mobilization of resources within the business community has even greater long-term significance for the new political order. In a mood that one executive described as "a siege mentality," brought on by increasing government regulation and a post-Watergate lack of public confidence, big business moved formally in 1974 to establish a new, militant, direct-lobbying organization, the Business Roundtable. Composed of 190 chief executive officers (CEOs) of major corporations such as General Motors, General Electric, DuPont, IBM, and AT&T, the Business Roundtable had become "the most powerful voice of business" by the end of 1976, according to *Business Week*. The Roundtable operates

New York and Washington offices and some support services; its operating expenses in 1981 were approximately $2.5 million. But its major resource is the commitment of its member CEOs, who lobby members of Congress and administration officials face-to-face. (The Roundtable has evolved a powerful "super-structure," consisting of a public-information committee composed of the public-relations officers of its member corporations, an economic-research committee of corporate economists, and a labor-management committee of industrial relations vice presidents.) A California Business Roundtable was subsequently organized by Justin Dart and David Packard.

The formation of the Business Roundtable, according to Leonard Silk and Mark Silk in *The American Establishment*, is a symbol of the rightward shift of business during the past decade. Roundtable member James Ferguson, board chairman of General Foods, explains: "Business was getting kicked around compared to labor, consumers, and other groups, and the constant cry within the business community was, 'How come we can't get together and make our voices heard?'" Business discovered it has power and "it is using that power."

To some extent this new business militancy was consciously encouraged by conservatives, and to some extent it was a relatively independent development that fortuitously complemented conservative activities. But the Business Roundtable's early and close relationship with AEI should be noted. Sidney Blumenthal quotes a Roundtable official: "It used to be that practically every policy committee meeting would talk about making contributions to support AEI."

The new corporate political involvement does not stop with the Business Roundtable. One recent development is the institutionalization of the "public affairs" function within the corporation, usually in the office of a vice president. The Public Affairs Council, based in Washington, is a professional service organization for this segment of the corporate community. Besides sponsoring conferences, the council publishes a journal, *Public Affairs Review*. According to Raymond Hoewing, council vice president, there are at least 800 corporate public-affairs units, 400 of which have been established in the past fifteen years. During the 1970s, "a decade of institutionalization," the number of corporate personnel in this field has at least tripled, in Hoewing's estimate.

Another new trend is toward opening a corporate Washington office. In an August 1978 cover story on Washington lobbyists, *Time* estimated that corporate offices in Washington had increased over the previous ten-year period from 100 to more than 500. In addition, 27 percent of the 6,000 national trade and professional associations which service an even larger corporate constituency had a Washington base.

The growth of advocacy advertising during the past few years has been remarkable. Mobil Oil Corporation, known as "America's most outspoken corporation," has taken the lead with a $4.5 million annual budget for issue advertising. (In 1982, Mobil's total public-relations budget, administered by vice president Herb Schmertz, was reported at $22 million, of which about $3 million went to public television and the Mobil Showcase. Sally Quinn of *The Washington Post* describes Schmertz as "the most powerful, most successful public-relations man in America," with a personal network in the media and liberal community. One high-visibility Mobil project in Washington is the National Town Meeting on various public-policy topics, held weekly at the John F. Kennedy Center.) Other corporations have followed Mobil's lead, including Amway, American Cyanamid, Bethlehem Steel, and United Technologies. One striking example of advocacy advertising was a W. R. Grace and Company ad in mid-1981 to respond to a *Washington Post* editorial that had criticized the

Reagan tax plan. (President Reagan later named Grace to head a private sector "cost control survey" of the federal government.) Other examples are provided by Smith Kline and LTV, which regularly publish full-page newspaper ads and multi-page magazine spreads on various public-policy issues. In 1980, LTV, and AEI pooled resources in the preparation of a series of *Wall Street Journal* ads and a book, *The Candidates 1980: Where They Stand.* A series of Supreme Court decisions since the mid-1970s has extended constitutional protection to the corporation's right of free speech, including campaign contributions. Its 1978 decision *First National Bank* v. *Bellotti* held that the First Amendment protects the speech of corporations exactly as it does the speech of individuals.

One of the most visible and controversial extensions of corporate power has been the proliferation of corporate political action committees (PACs) that followed changes in campaign spending regulations in the mid-1970s. At the end of 1974 there were 89 corporate PACs in the United States. The total increased dramatically to 433 by the end of 1976, and continued to expand to 1,512 as of July 1983, according to the Federal Election Commission (FEC). (The total number, including trade-union and issue-oriented PACs, grew from roughly 600 to 3,371 over the same period.) An important effect of the change in campaign spending regulations has been to divert contributions from the now federally subsidized presidential primary and general elections to congressional and state campaigns. The FEC estimates that total PAC spending for congressional candidates increased from $21 million in 1976 to $35 million in 1978 to $60 million in 1980; corporate PACs spent $87.3 million on the 1981–82 congressional elections. "PACs are a corrosive force at the heart of the political process," claims Common Cause president Fred Wertheimer, who favors excluding all private money from electoral politics. While the

FEC and groups like Common Cause monitor contributions at the federal level, PAC contributions to state and local candidates are generally not reported unless required by those jurisdictions.

The corporate PAC movement has also emphasized state politics, especially in California, Texas, Illinois, and Ohio. Representatives of eighty-eight major corporations and trade associations have organized the State Government Affairs Council, which has developed relationships with the National Conference of State Legislatures and the National Governors' Association. Corporate political organization at the state level parallels the development of the New Right network and the American Legislative Exchange Council.

Certain corporations have taken the lead in the PAC movement. In the fall of 1979, the International Association of Machinists (IAM) filed a 45-page complaint with the FEC, charging a number of corporate PACs, including those of Dart Industries, Eaton, General Electric, General Motors, Grumman, International Paper, Union Camp, Union Oil of California, United Technologies, and Winn-Dixie, with using coercive methods of fund-raising. Justin Dart of Dart Industries has been called "the Johnny Appleseed of the corporate PAC movement" because of his travels around the country, persuading corporate leaders to start or expand their own PACs.

Greg Denier, a former IAM staff member who has researched the corporate political movement, argues that corporate PACs and the New Right are closely allied. "The New Right's primary purpose," observes Denier, "is to fund candidates and to run their campaigns. . . . The corporate and trade association PACs are to come through with the money." This specialization of function allows business leaders to stay above party politics, primary fights, and precinct organization.

At the same time, the availability of the "right" candidate

complements the strategy of corporate groups like BIPAC, the Business/Industry Political Action Committee, which is actively "attempting to change the philosophic makeup of Congress." The National Association of Manufacturers (NAM), which has strong New Right ties, publishes a newsletter, *The PAC Manager*, providing "decision-making information for PAC administrators," including lists of candidates endorsed by BIPAC and a PAC calendar listing public-affairs council meetings, BIPAC briefings, and PAC exchange council seminars. This suggests the extensive informal communications network that functions within the corporate PAC movement.

Even more important than the proliferation of corporate PACs is the quiet corporate development of grass-roots political organizations. More than 260 major corporations have already established grass-roots political involvement and education programs to complement the top-level lobbying of groups like the Business Roundtable. In the lead are Arco, Burlington Industries, U.S. Steel, Mead, Inland Container, and Dart Industries. The Chamber of Commerce and NAM also have national programs to coordinate the constituency efforts of individual companies. One veteran public-affairs official assigns a relative weight of 50 points to CEO lobbying (the Business Roundtable), 30 points to grass-roots organization, and only 20 points to PAC contributions, suggesting the priorities of corporate political investment.

A dramatic example of how the new corporate lobbying organization works away from public view is provided by the Senate vote supporting Reagan on the AWACS sale in 1981. At the time, the national media focused on the President's role in changing the votes of key senators, calling him "the man with the golden arm." The corporate lobbying effort that supported him was scarcely mentioned until *The New Republic* published an investigative report by Steven Emerson in mid-

February 1982. Emerson documented "a massive and unprecedented corporate lobbying campaign" devised by a five-member Saudi–U.S. group including Prince Bandar bin Sultan and former Democratic party professional Frederick Dutton. Representatives of forty corporations, primarily in defense, aerospace, and petroleum-related industries, met regularly with a White House staff member at the Washington offices of the Business Roundtable to coordinate strategy.

Boeing, the prime contractor on the AWACS project, and United Technologies generated what Emerson describes as "one of the most successful chain-letter operations in history," sending more than 10,000 telegrams to subsidiaries, vendors, subcontractors, suppliers, and distributors across the country. Recipients were asked to write their two U.S. senators and send a copy to corporate headquarters. The result was a torrent of thousands of letters and Washington visits by local delegations of executives. An interesting feature of the campaign was the involvement of a number of corporations that had no substantial business interests in Saudi Arabia, including John Deere, Republic Steel, Alcoa Aluminium, Smith Kline, Pepsi-Cola, and even the Florist Insurance Companies. On the morning of the AWACS vote, a group of twenty-three corporate leaders, including IBM chairman emeritus Thomas J. Watson, Jr., signed a telex from Riyadh to individual senators, capping the successful drive.

Instead of reacting to legislative and regulatory problems as they arise, business now helps to shape the evolving political debate on an issue. The leading business research and policy organization, the Committee for Economic Development (CED), typically researches issues two to five years before they become visible. (Silk and Silk describe CED's role in introducing Keynesian economics to the business community in the 1940s. Today the CED serves as a moderating influence on the

Business Roundtable through overlapping membership. CED also maintains contact with the conservative think tanks: Rudolph G. Penner, a resident scholar at AEI, serves on the CED Research Advisory Board.)

The business press, including *The Wall Street Journal, Fortune, Business Week, Forbes,* and *Barrons,* provides a natural forum for issue development and discussion within the business community. Its connections with the new conservative intelligentsia are extensive. Since 1972, under the leadership of Robert L. Bartley, *The Wall Street Journal* editorial and op-ed pages have become a "sort of national bulletin board for political and military commentary by the network of conservative and neoconservative intellectuals and . . . policymakers," noted Dan Morgan of *The Washington Post. Fortune* regularly features articles by conservative intellectuals.

Perhaps the leading example of the business influence in formulating policy issues is the theme of "the reindustrialization of America," which received its major statement in a special issue of *Business Week* on June 30, 1980. The *Business Week* analysis documented the decline of U.S. industry, and its causes; the need for "a new social contract" backed by support from business, labor, and government; and a new national industrial policy to encourage the growth sectors of the economy. The document had political implications, including a call for lowering "expectations that can no longre be met." (The list of "attitudes that helped undermine growth" paralleled the neoconservative critique of New Deal social policy: "The notion of entitlement, a new definition of equality that called on government to level economic and social disparities, an adversary stance toward government and business, and changed motivations toward work.")

While there were some disagreements within the business community, especially over the degree of government involvement, the reindustrialization-of-America theme was echoed in a remarkable media blitz. Walter H. Annenberg published an editorial commentary in *TV Guide*, reprinted as a full-page ad in *The Wall Street Journal*. Emphasizing the need for higher productivity, Annenberg stated, "This article itself is a direct plea to the electorate to understand the facts behind what may well be the most important issue of the coming campaign, and to the candidates to address this issue directly." Chase Manhattan ran several full-page *Journal* ads in subsequent weeks. *Newsweek* presented a cover story, "The Productivity Crisis: Can America Renew Its Economic Purpose?" in its September 8, 1980, issue. *U.S. News & World Report* followed two weeks later with a cover story, "Rebuilding America: It Will Cost Trillions." NBC-TV provided a Reuven Frank "White Paper" called "If Japan Can . . . Why Can't We?" Even Harvard University picked up the refrain as a co-sponsor (with the New York Stock Exchange and the U.S. Senate Subcommittee on International Trade) of a conference, "Can the United States Remain Competitive?" with a full-page "consensus statement" also appearing in the *Journal*.

Free enterprise and free-market economics are the subjects of a public-relations and education effort by the business community. Corporations have funded at least forty professorships of free enterprise at American colleges and universities. The Advertising Council spent several million dollars on a campaign to promote the free-enterprise system. The Milton Friedman PBS series, *Free to Choose*, a primer in free-market economics, was financed by a consortium of conservative foundations and corporations. Phillips Petroleum has invested $800,000 in a five-film series on *American Enterprise*, which has been seen by more than 8 million students. A National Leadership Institute based in Austin, Texas, runs competitive statewide seminars, "Students in Free Enterprise." The American Economic Foundation monitors high-school economics textbooks from a free-enterprise perspective. Individual conservative like Justin Dart have also made a major contribution to free-enterprise education. Dart's Enterprise America, based in Los Angeles, has printed and distributed more than 2 million copies of William Simon's *A Time for Action* as it was condensed by the *Reader's Digest*.

The political dimension of this campaign is illustrated by one of the most interesting conservative organizations, the Law and Economics Center of Atlanta's Emory University (formerly located at the University of Miami School of Law). The Law and Economics Center owes its success to the entrepreneurial genius of its founder, Henry G. Manne, and to more than 200 conservative and corporate donors. (L&EC has ties to the network on both points. Manne serves on other boards including those of The Media Institute, a business-funded organization in Washington, the anti-Nader American Council on Science and Health, and the Reason Foundation in California. Conservative donors to L&EC include the Boulware Trust, Adolph Coors Company and Foundation, Dart Industries, the Liberty Fund, John M. Olin Foundation, various Scaife family foundations, the DeWitt Wallace [Reader's Digest] Fund and Edwin J. Feulner of the Heritage Foundation.) L&EC operates a series of institutes and seminars, including an economics institute for law professors, a legal institute for economists, and an economics institute for congressional staff aides, all aimed at providing a more sophisticated understanding of the interplay of economics, politics, and the law to elite groups. The center's most widely sold publication, *The Attack on Corporate America,* examines criticism of large corporations and of American corporate capitalism from a pro-business perspective.

The jewel in the crown of L&EC's educational programs is

the economics institute for federal judges, a two-week course in market theory inaugurated in December 1976. By the end of 1980, 137 federal district and circuit judges had completed the basic institute and 56 had returned for an advanced third week in quantitative methods or antitrust economics. A *Fortune* cover story (May 21, 1979), "Judges Get a Crash Course in Economics," described the program. Instructors, drawn "almost to a man" from the free-market school of economics, exposed students to tools of microeconomic analysis like marginal cost and utility curves, detached as much as possible from "normative judgments." While the judges gave the program a generally favorable verdict, some balked at the effort to reduce complex realities to simple market economics. One judge, for example, voiced concern at the analysis of conglomerates, arguing "that the centralization of economic power will lead to a centralization of political power." But a recent L&EC publication contains glowing testimonials from nine (unnamed) federal judges. (The author heard another judge tell a group of business and professional people how he had used economic analysis learned at L&EC in writing some of his opinions.)

Like many other labyrinth organizations, L&EC has ambitious plans for expansion. The John M. Olin Foundation has funded a fellowship program in law and economics, enabling trained economists to pursue three years of interdisciplinary study leading to a JD degree at the center. A second center journal, devoted to the analysis of selected U.S. Supreme Court decisions from an economic perspective, is planned. A Ph.D. program in law and economics, a health-policy program, and a special fellowship program for scholars outside the fields of law and economics are also projected.

Another indication of the more aggressive political posture of American business is stronger opposition to organized labor. The March 1977 defeat in the House of Representatives of legislation to legalize common-site picketing in the construction industry was a major defeat for labor and a success for the business-conservative coalition. Principal elements in the coalition were the Business Roundtable, the U.S. Chamber of Commerce, the National Right to Work Committee, and Associated General Contractors. *Congressional Quarterly* credited an "intensive and well-managed indirect lobbying" campaign by the Chamber of Commerce and NRTWC, using computer targeting and direct mail, as crucial in the defeat of the bill.

The role of NRTWC in the coalition deserves special note. NRTWC's major purpose is to oppose the closed shop or what it calls "compulsory unionization." It supports Section 14(b) of the Taft-Hartley Act of 1947, which allows states to ban the closed shop. Twenty states, mostly in the South, currently have such laws, and the American Legislative Exchange Council encourages their spread through one of its model statutes. NRTWC is involved in a wide range of anti-union efforts, including opposition to labor-supported legislation for election-day voter registration and public financing of congressional campaigns. NRTWC president Reed Larson made defeat of the common-site picketing bill a special project of the committee, allocating $750,000 to a direct-mail and newspaper advertising campaign. The committee placed full-page ads in fifty newspapers in seventeen targeted states. While nominally independent of the business community, NRTWC also participated in the National Action Committee on Secondary Boycotts, which coordinated opposition strategy.

Under Larson's leadership, NRTWC has spun off a number of interconnected anti-union organizations which Thomas B. Mechling described as "business fronts of the far, far right" in *Business and Society Review*. In 1974, Larson helped organize the Public Service Research Council (PSRC), which subsequently developed a subsidiary, Americans Against Union

Control of Government (AAUCG). The scale of the NRTWC and PSRC direct-mail operations is staggering. NRTWC, which refers to itself as "a coalition of employers and employees 1,750,000 strong," operated on an annual budget of almost $9 million. Its staff of over 100 generates 25 million computerized letters per year, a volume so large that NRTWC has been assigned its own zip code in Virginia (22038)! Over a three-year period in the mid-1970s, NRTWC increased its contributing membership from 27,000 to 360,000. The more recently organized PSRC has experienced a similar growth with a budget of $3.5 million, a staff of 30, and contributions from more than 500,000 individuals as of 1982. The direct-mail expertise behind NRTWC and PSRC comes from James L. Martin, who was an apprentice with the Viguerie organization.

Thomas Mechling, who studied groups like NRTWC, PSRC, and AAUCG, says that they "show an ability to adapt new symbols and semantics to old Birchite views" and are "able to make use of the most advanced fund-raising and propagandizing techniques." He argues that "there is good reason to suspect that the legitimate views and fears of conservative citizens are being secretly manipulated by still-anonymous businesses and businessmen" who have set up and supported these anti-union groups.

Yet another dimension of the anti-union drive is the growth of what Herbert E. Meyer of *Fortune* described as "a mini-industry of consulting firms [that] has arisen to help companies prepare and, when necessary, implement strike contingency plans." Philadelphia attorney Stephen J. Cabot, profiled in a front-page *Wall Street Journal* story, exemplifies these consultants, who specialize in helping management win an increasing percentage of the elections that determine union representation. "Today's labor-relations consultants," commented the late George Meany, "carry briefcases instead of brass knuckles"—and to labor's dismay, they are far more effective. The big news in labor-management warfare, concluded Meyer, is "the new, increasingly militant posture of management," which parallels an observable drop in public support for unions and strikes.

The corporate sector's new involvement in politics is nowhere better illustrated than in the transformation of the U.S. Chamber of Commerce from "a stodgy business federation" to what one *Fortune* writer has described as "a mass movement with at least the semblance of a guiding ideology—an organization that seems more political party than lobby." In 1983, the Chamber of Commerce had a national budget of $65 million for research, communications, and political activities—three times what it was in 1974. (State and local chambers of commerce spent tens of millions beyond that. These figures are substantially higher than the combined budgets for the Republican and Democratic National Committees.) The central figure in the growth of the Chamber of Commerce is Richard Lesher, who was hired from NASA by Pepsico chairman Donald Kendall in 1971 and nominated for the Chamber presidency in 1975 by Kendall and fellow board members August Busch III, Joseph Coors, and William May of American Can. Lesher has expanded the Chamber's grass-roots network of 1,400 congressional action committees to more than 2,700. In 1977, the Chamber of Commerce added to its "public-interest" lobby Citizen's Choice (chaired by Jay Van Andel of Amway), which had at that time enrolled 76,000 individuals apart from local chambers and business groups. Today the Citizen's Choice hotline telephone network can generate 12,000 phone calls to legislators within twenty-four hours. The Chamber has its own political action committee, the National Chamber Alliance for Politics, and a small public-interest law firm. The National Chamber Foundation is a tax-exempt affiliate which sponsor projects like Corporate Philanthropy in the Eighties (the proceedings of a conference co-sponsored with the California Chamber of Commerce in September 1979). The U.S. Chamber of Commerce syndicates a weekly TV debate show, *It's Your Business*, to 158 stations around the country. Its two-way closed-circuit television network, Biznet, links local chambers and corporations via satellite with headquarters in Washington. Several cable networks carry *Biznet News Today*. Its development strategy, similar to that of AEI, involves a five-year capital campaign, inaugurated in 1981, to raise $30 million to $60 million in one-time gifts.

Veteran Democratic representative Richard Bolling of Missouri notes that the Chamber has "always been the effective core of the conservative coalition." The new Chamber of Commerce, along with the new development of business political organization, suggests massive investments of money that are helping to finance a new political order.

7

Conservatives in Congress: Anything within the Rules Is Fair Game

THE CONTRAST between the Republican old guard that controlled the Senate in the early 1950s—Taft, Jenner, Knowland, et al.—and the New Right legislators in the Senate and House today is a striking indication of the profound changes in American politics.

The conservative right steadily and systematically increased its numbers on Capitol Hill during the 1960s and 1970s. Conservative organizations helped to recruit, fund, and elect members of Congress from their ranks who have used their offices to help build the movement. Examples include Representatives Philip M. Crane (R–Illinois), who has served as chair of the American Conservative Union (ACU), and Mickey Edwards (R–Oklahoma), ACU treasurer, not to mention the clutch of New Right senators elected in the mid- and late 1970s who regularly sign Viguerie fund-raising letters. "Many of these people have been working together for ten to twenty years in youth groups," observes Robert Bauman, a conservative Republican member of Congress from Maryland from 1973 to 1980, and one of the founders of Young Americans for Freedom.

The new conservatives have developed and staffed their own

organizations within the congressional Republican Party. In the House, the Republican Study Committee was formed in the early 1970s. Modeled on the liberal Democratic Study Group, it included 130 of the party's 167 House members by 1983. Edwin J. Feulner served as its executive director before becoming president of the Heritage Foundation. A counterpart conservative Steering Committee was established in the Senate by Senator Carl T. Curtis (R–Nebraska) and eight other Republican senators, including Jesse Helms, in April 1974. The Senate Steering Committee, attacked by Democratic Majority Leader Senator Robert C. Byrd in 1979 as a "shadowy," "mysterious" organization, now has at least twenty core members from the new Republican majority. Attendance at its recent meetings ran as high as twenty-five to thirty. Its staff of four helps coordinate legislative activities and plan strategy.

The Steering Committee has succeeded in electing Senator James McClure to the number-three leadership position in the Republican majority—chairman of the Senate Republican Conference—and in placing its members in a range of Senate committee and subcommittee chairs important to the advancement of New Right social legislation. One of the more controversial appointments has been Judiciary chairman Strom Thurmond's selection of retired Admiral Jeremiah Denton, Jr. (R–Alabama), founder of the Coalition for Decency, a Helms-Weyrich protégé and new member of the Steering Committee, to head the new Subcommittee on Security and Terrorism.

One of the major obstacles to conservative efforts to establish a new political majority in the United States has been the Democrats' long domination of Congress. The Democratic Party controlled both houses of Congress and their powerful committee systems, without interruption, from 1956 to 1980. Ironically, the Goldwater nomination in 1964, which was supposed to offer the American voter "a choice, not an echo," produced the greatest Democratic majorities since the 1930s and the famous 89th Congress (1965–66), which enacted the full backlog of New Deal legislation blocked for years by the conservative coalition—Lyndon Johnson's Great Society. Republicans argue that one-party domination has led to abuses of power and an arrogant attitude on the part of the Democratic leadership.

Efforts to loosen Democratic control of the Congress met their first major success in 1980, when the Republicans won control of the Senate. The media focused on the defeat of senior liberal Democratic senators who had been targeted by the New Right, notably Birch Bayh (Indiana), Frank Church (Idaho), and George McGovern (South Dakota). Less noticed was the fact that the Republicans had effectively stolen a page from Democratic campaign strategists. In the 1950s, the liberal National Committee for an Effective Congress (NCEC) devised a strategy to defeat McCarthy Republicans in the Senate. NCEC channeled money into Senate races in sparsely populated states in the West, helping to launch liberal candidates like Frank Church. (NCEC had discovered the so-called cheapies, states where relatively small sums of money could influence the election of Democratic senators.) In view of the normal Republican presidential majority since Nixon's presidency in states west of the Mississippi, it was only a matter of time until Republican strategists caught up with NCEC. The electoral arithmetic suggests that Republicans may dominate the U.S. Senate for the rest of this century.

The political balance of the Senate has been shifted both by the removal of prominent liberal Democrats with years of seniority and by the addition of several New Right senators, most of whom have been quickly assimilated into the conservative Steering Committee. Liberal Republican decline was signaled by the primary defeat of Senator Jacob K. Javits of

New York by conservative Alfonse M. D'Amato (although Javits's failing health was an important issue in the campaign), following the 1978 primary defeat of Senator Clifford Case of New Jersey by a New Right candidate. Even more important has been the shift in party control of the committees and committee staffs of the Senate. For decades, the Democrats have used the professional staffs of Congress as a source of talent and policy ideas. Literally hundreds of staff positions are now available to Republicans and conservatives. The full impact of the shift in committee control remains to be seen.

The House of Representatives has proved a tougher nut for the Republicans and conservatives to crack. Here the Democrats enjoy the advantages of incumbency and gerrymandering. In 1980, Republican candidates won 50.2 percent of the two-party vote but only 41 percent of the House seats. (Democratic control of state legislatures allowed the party to redraw congressional district boundaries in its favor following the censuses of 1960, 1970, and 1980.) While Democrats gained in the 1982 congressional elections on the strength of Reagan's problems with the economy, Republicans have evolved a long-term strategy for winning the House. According to Nancy Sinnet, former head of the Republican Congressional Campaign Committee, Republican committees pooled a record $60 million in campaign funds for the 1982 elections. The Republican National Committee has invested several million dollars in the redistricting fight over several years, retaining consulting organizations like Market Opinion Research Company of Detroit to develop computer programs for Republican state organizations. (The California Business Roundtable made a similar investment of $600,000 in redistricting studies by the Rose Institute of State and Local Government in Claremont, California. In addition to monitoring redistricting in California, the Rose Institute has sold its services in other important states, such as Illinois, Texas, and Pennsylvania.) The Republicans have also initiated a campaign for a Republican Congress using sophisticated political ads on national television. Some $10 million was budgeted for TV advertising in 1982.

One Republican option that should be watched carefully is the so-called coalitions strategy that Paul Weyrich has been promoting. Even without victory against the Democrats at the polls, Republicans could break the Democratic majority within the House through party switches. In October 1981, House Democrats were stunned when Pennsylvania Democratic representative Eugene V. Atkinson appeared at a news conference with President Reagan in the White House Rose Garden to announce his defection to the Republican Party. Atkinson, running as a Republican, was defeated in 1982. A second Democrat, Bob Stump of Arizona, had announced a few weeks earlier that he would become a Republican in the next Congress. Phil Gramm of Texas resigned from the House when fellow Democrats expelled him from the House Budget Committee because of his support of Reagan's economic policies. In February 1983 he won a special election and returned to Congress as a Republican. House Republican whip Trent Lott of Mississippi has said that as many as a dozen House Democrats are considering moving to the Republican side. Prime prospects include some of the forty-seven House members of the Conservative Democratic Forum (primarily Southern Democrats, the so-called Boll Weevils), especially the twenty-three "triple defectors" who voted with Reagan on the two crucial budget votes and the tax vote in 1981. Larry P. McDonald, the Bircher from Georgia who worked closely with the New Right before his death in September 1983, was frequently mentioned as a potential switcher. "I've heard almost every moderate and conservative Democrat up here talking about whether they might switch parties," McDonald told *Congressional Quarterly* in late 1981.

The rumor of impending party switches is partly psychological warfare, but such talk should not be dismissed lightly. Before the 1980 elections, *National Review* announced that "if the GOP gets within grabbing distance of Senate control, there are several conservative Democrats who just might pop across the aisle and midwife that late-emerging Republican majority." As it happened, the Republicans had no need to call on Harry Byrd, Fritz Hollings, John Stennis, and Edward Zorinsky, the magazine's prime prospects. House Republicans, however, may need to exercise that option. To many political professionals, Democratic loss of control of the House of Representatives seems a remote possibility. But were it to occur, it would have a traumatic effect on the Democratic Party establishment, far beyond the 1980 loss of the Senate.

Congressional party rivalries may seem like politics as usual. However, the conservatives within Republican ranks are changing congressional politics in at least two fundamental ways— political style and extra-congressional organizations. As self-proclaimed radicals intent on restructuring American politics, they must be taken seriously. Besides, as Wes McCune of Group Research observed, "It is well advertised that the GOP now controls the Senate. But it is still not realized that the right wing controls the GOP."

The new conservatives have introduced their own version of "hardball" politics in the Senate and House. New Right senators like Orrin G. Hatch and Jake Garn of Utah have pressed the filibuster to new limits. Jesse Helms has promised his national direct-mail constituency "never to leave the floor of the Senate unattended by one of us." In the House, Robert Bauman, during his tenure, pioneered uses of House rules for blocking the House Democratic leadership. Senator Garn sums up the change in style: "My attitude is, anything within the rules is fair game." *Congressional Quarterly* observes that many of the new conservatives "arrive in Washington with stronger loyalties to national conservative politics than to Congress as an institution, or to the Republican Party." The concern of congressional professionals is not unlike that of Republican regulars who witnessed the takeover of the party organization by the Goldwater conservatives in the 1960s. Commenting on the Senate Steering Committee and the supporting network of Senate aides, political analyst Peter Ross Range concluded, "This kind of coordination is almost unprecedented in Senate history."

The conservative development of extra-congressional organizations from within Congress is also new in scale. As has often been the case, a technique invented by liberals was copied by conservatives and raised to new levels of effectiveness by ample funding. Frustrated by the conservative coalition, and especially by the seniority of Southerners within the Democratic congressional party, liberal Democrats in the House in the late 1950s banded together, with encouragement from NCEC, to form the Democratic Study Group (DSG). In addition to improving internal House operations (communications, whip counts, research, and policy), the DSG put its campaign fundraising and strategy capability at the service of liberal Democrats across the country. Tax-exempt groups like the Taconic Foundation also functioned as part of the DSG network. This "outside the House" strategy reached fruition in the mid-1970s, when liberal Democrats overthrew several senior chairs and "democratized" the party's rules within the House and its committees. The DSG was largely funded by individual members of Congress, who donated part of their staff salary allowances. This arrangement was adopted by a variety of what we could call "congressional action groups" during the 1960s and 1970s, from the Black Caucus to the Republican Study Committee and Senate Steering Committee.

In the ten years he has spent in the U.S. Senate, Jesse Helms has used his Senate office to build an extra-congressional organization without equal in American politics. A *Congressional Quarterly* special report (March 6, 1982) concluded: "Like no other senator in history, Helms and his lieutenants have used modern technology and expert knowledge of federal election and tax law to erect a network of political organizations bent on influencing politics and policy." With a personal following on the political right second in size only to that of Ronald Reagan, and more ideologically committed, Helms and his personal and institutional history are inevitably part of the story of the conservative labyrinth.

We can identify some half dozen branches of the Helms network. First is Helms's top-level congressional staff, including John Carbaugh and James Lucier, who were recruited from the Strom Thurmond organization. *Time* has described the Helms inner group as "a squad of smart, youngish devotees more ruthlessly conservative, if that is possible, than he." Carbaugh and Lucier are the top professionals in what has been referred to as Helms's "shadow State Department." The two flew to Africa and London at the expense of the Helms organization to lobby for the white-minority regime of Ian Smith during the Rhodesia-Zimbabwe peace talks. Carbaugh, who organized the Madison Group, the top-level conservative foreign-policy staff network, has been implicated in several foreign-policy "leaks" designed to embarrass Helms's opponents. "Carbaugh is a kind of bandit for Helms," stated Peter Ross Range, "the sort of guy who can throw bombs all over Washington while giving his boss the comfortable shield of deniability." Less well known is Carbaugh's connection with the New Right. Howard Phillips, as a part-time Helms worker, used the Helms Senate office as a base for launching the conservative grass-roots organization, The Conservative Caucus. Carbaugh claims to have invented both The Conservative Caucus and Terry Dolan's National Conservative Political Action Committee in Helms's office, reported Range. Carbaugh left the Helms staff in the summer of 1982 to join the new Washington law firm of Vance, Joyce and Carbaugh. He maintains connections with Helms and expects to continue to "put in my two cents all over the place."

Carbaugh, Lucier, and other Helms staff members operate a second branch of the Helms empire—a half dozen non-profit educational foundations based in Washington and Raleigh, North Carolina. The four Helms tax-exempt foundations in Washington—The Institute of American Relations and its Foreign Affairs Council; the American Family Institute; the Center for a Free Society; and the Institute on Money and Inflation—had a combined budget of about $2.5 million in 1979–80. (Nelson Bunker Hunt is the largest supporter of the IAR, contributing $90,000 between 1976 and 1979.) Together with the Congressional Club Foundation and the Coalition for Freedom in Raleigh, the "institutes" undertake research and education across the full spectrum of social, economic, and national security and foreign policy issues. The Institute of American Relations produces a semimonthly foreign policy newsletter, *American Relations*; the American Family Institute funded a trip to Washington in June 1981 for Nobel Prize winner Mother Teresa of Calcutta, to participate in a seminar on the family with conservative theorists like George Gilder; the Coalition for Freedom has produced a half-hour film on national defense; the Institute of American Relations sponsored national public-opinion surveys on the Panama Canal treaties. While the scale of the Institute's activities does not match the major conservative think tanks like AEI or Heritage, it is unique in congressional annals.

A third element of the Helms network is the National Congressional Club, the Helms PAC based in Raleigh and directed by Helms's senior political adviser, attorney Tom Ellis. The Congressional Club began after the 1972 Senate campaign, when Ellis retained Richard Viguerie to help pay off the Helms campaign debt. Ellis and Viguerie built the Congressional Club mailing list to more than 300,000 regular contributors—a constituency for Helms and a major financial resource within the conservative movement. In 1978, when Helms ran for reelection, the club helped to raise what is still a record expenditure for a U.S. Senate campaign—more than $7.5 million. (The New Right participated extensively in the 1978 campaign, and we can reasonably assume that some of that record sum went into other conservative organizations. In 1979 the Congressional Club formally became a "multi-candidate committee," a PAC contributing to the election of candidates other than Helms. Another New Right candidate, Robert Dornan of California, holds the record for the most expensive House campaign—$1.9 million in 1980.) The Congressional Club generates between 10 and 20 million letters a year, and in 1982 raised $4.5 million, maintaining its position as the largest PAC in the country. Until 1983, it ran a Washington office to "help us maintain communications with conservatives in Congress and other conservative groups," according to executive director Carter Wrenn.

Finally, a new tier of political organizations has been created by Helms's aides with the assistance of the Washington establishment law firm of Covington and Burling. Jefferson Marketing, Inc., was set up in Raleigh in 1978 as a political consulting, advertising, and direct-mail company in tandem with the Congressional Club. The firm can legally assist candidates without violating the campaign limits that govern PACs. A separate bookkeeping firm, the Hardison Corporation, was formed to file reports from the Congressional Club and other Helms political satellites, like the Jesse for Vice President Committee (now defunct) with the Federal Election Commission. Jefferson Marketing and Hardison are innovations that do not fall under federal election law and, accordingly, need not file financial reports with the FEC. As a result, the Congressional Club is able to channel large sums of money to Jefferson Marketing ($2.1 million between 1979 and mid-1981) in the form of consulting fees, payments for services, and expense reimbursements, with no further indication of where the funds are going. The unique freedom of the Helms political machine from campaign spending regulations, geographical boundaries, and even party loyalties is new in American politics.

Helms has used his political organization to build connections with New Right and conservative political activists. Besides the Viguerie, Phillips, and Dolan connections, Helms is actively represented in Weyrich's coordinating groups. As the chairman of the Senate Steering Committee, Helms is the chief legislative strategist for the conservative social agenda. His American Family Institute and its president, Carl Anderson (who accepted Reagan's appointment to the Health and Human Services Department in June 1981), are part of the conservative "pro-family" movement. Helms also occupies a central position in the religious right as a member of the Religious Roundtable, a lay preacher, and a former radio and television political evangelist.

Helms's segregationist past and current advocacy of white supremacist regimes in South Africa make him a natural leader of Southern segregationists. *Time* characterized his 2,700 TV editorial transcripts as "packed with hyperbole and mean-spiritedness. Yet, perhaps because this was television, he never crossed the line into ugliness or outright racism—as some Tobacco Network listeners seem to remember he did in his early radio talks (of which no transcripts are known to exist)." Tom Ellis is a former director of the Pioneer Fund, which conducts research to demonstrate the genetic inferiority of blacks. Unlike former segregationist Strom Thurmond, Helms has not hired blacks on his Senate staff.

Helms has used the Steering Committee and two vice-presidential campaigns to push the Republican Party platforms of 1976 and 1980 farther right. New Right strategist Paul Weyrich credits Helms with forcing dozens of roll-call votes on social issues in the Senate. "With those votes we were able to pin the pro-abortion, pro-busing, pro-pornography, pro-whatever label on those senators who otherwise would have gotten away with those views for years and years to come." Helms and Ellis effectively saved Ronald Reagan's political career in 1976 by staging a Reagan upset victory in the North Carolina Republican primary, just when President Gerald Ford seemed to be on the verge of a political knockout. Like many other conservatives, Helms's loyalty is not to the Republican Party but to the conservative cause. "We are a bridge between conservative Democrats and conservative Republicans," comments strategist Ellis. "I would like to see a realignment under the Republican banner, but it wouldn't bother me to change the name." For all its power, though, the Helms organization should not be overrated. The senator could be defeated by popular North Carolina Democratic governor, James B. Hunt, in 1984.

Another power base to watch is the rapidly developing political organization of New York Republican congressman Jack Kemp. New Right political consultant Roger Stone is coordinating direct-mail and $1,000-a-head fund-raising events to support Kemp's new political action committee, the Campaign for Prosperity, designed to generate grass-roots support for Reaganomics and financial contributions for Republican congressional candidates, and the related American Renaissance Foundation, which sponsors research and conferences, including one on international monetary policy in May 1983. Political professionals see Kemp as the heir apparent to the Reagan wing of the Republican Party. Kemp's PAC allows him to campaign for other Republicans around the country: Justin Dart; Joseph Coors; William Batten, chairman of the New York Stock Exchange; Leon Hess of Amerada Hess; Roger Milliken of Deering-Milliken textiles; and other corporate leaders head the list of early contributors ($250,000 in 1980) to the Kemp PAC.

In summer 1982, Kemp, who edits a bimonthly supply-side newsletter for the Fund for a Conservative Majority (*The Congressman Jack Kemp Report*), organized an open conservative revolt against the Reagan plan to raise $98.9 billion in new taxes to reduce the federal deficit. Among the thirty conservatives who joined Kemp in planning strategy, according to a report by *Time* magazine, were former Reagan treasury aides Paul Craig Roberts and Norman Ture, former White House aide Martin Anderson, Richard Viguerie, Howard Phillips, Irving Kristol, Pepsico chairman Don Kendall, and U.S. Chamber of Commerce president Richard Lesher. Representative Newt Gingrich (R–Georgia) characterized the Kemp revolt as the "opening round of the fight for the soul and future of the Republican Party."

8

The Republican Party Organization: A Wholly Owned Subsidiary

THE CONSERVATIVES must control the presidency as well as Congress to effect a realignment of American politics based on a "new [conservative] majority." This objective, in comparison to capture of the Congress, has been relatively easy to achieve. With the takeover of the party organization by supporters of Goldwater in 1964, Republican politics underwent a fundamental change. Some discussion of this critical period in American political history puts the conservative movement into fuller perspective.

The end of the Eisenhower presidency and the defeat of Richard Nixon in 1960 created a vacuum in Republican Party politics. To their surprise, Goldwater strategists like F. Clifton White and William Rusher discovered they were "pushing against an open door." In state after state, Goldwater activists took over party organizations and the machinery for nominating delegates to the Republican National Convention. By the time Rockefeller, Lodge, Romney, and Scranton forces realized what was happening, the Republican nomination and platform were firmly in the hands of the conservatives. Goldwater's defeat of Rockefeller in the 1964 California primary provided a decisive majority, although White could probably have engineered a convention majority even without the California delegation.

The Goldwater movement was unlike anything Republican Party regulars had ever seen. In many states longtime leaders, even former Taft supporters, were purged for questionable loyalty to the conservative cause. "Purists" replaced "politicians." With Goldwater's disastrous defeat in November 1964, the stage was set for a counterattack. Its immediate objective was to replace the pro-Goldwater Republican national chairman, Dean Burch, with Ohio's Republican leader, Ray C. Bliss, a party professional, at the Republican National Committee meeting in Chicago in January 1965.

Internal Republican Party politics since the mid-1960s can best be described as an unevenly balanced equilibrium between three factions on a roughly right-center-left spectrum—the ideological conservatives, the Republican Party regulars and traditional conservatives, and the Republican "moderates" (a term adopted during the 1960s as more acceptable than "liberal" or "progressive"). The 1968 nomination fight among Reagan, Nixon, and Rockefeller was perhaps the classic expression of this alignment. Lacking sufficient strength to nominate a chairman of their own, the moderates joined forces with the regulars to elect Bliss. Since then, the media have tended to depict Republican politics along the tripartite lines, with party centrists (Nixon, Ford, Bush) allied with moderates against party conservatives (Reagan in 1968, 1976, and 1980).

The picture is actually more complicated. With Nelson Rockefeller's last nomination bid in 1968, moderate Republican presidential politics effectively came to an end. The point cannot be stressed strongly enough, for this development, still not fully appreciated, profoundly skews all subsequent Republican Party politics. The moderate wing, since Rockefeller, has provided attractive national candidates with potential appeal to the political center and the large bloc of independent voters—governors like William Milliken of Michigan, Dan Evans of Washington, and Jim Thompson of Illinois; senators like Mark Hatfield of Oregon, Charles Percy of Illinois, and Edward W. Brooke of Massachusetts; and Cabinet- and subcabinet-level officers like Elliot Richardson and William Ruckelshaus. Yet not one Republican moderate has mounted a full presidential campaign since 1968. (George Bush was promoted as a moderate Republican candidate in 1980, but his voting record, conservative campaign manager [David Keene], AEI brain trust, and Texas oil money hardly qualify him as a moderate. Representative John Anderson, the only moderate Republican in the race, opted for an independent candidacy before the Republican convention.) When one considers that nominating (and general election) campaigns are the quadrennial means by which party factions renew their strength; train field staff, advance men, and political cadres; engage in party platform contests and convention maneuvering; and develop current lists of contributors, it becomes painfully clear that the moderate Republicans have for some time been out of the ball game. John Anderson's decision to go independent was a recognition of that reality. (Some of Anderson's supporters pleaded with him to stay in the party and, as Goldwater had done for the conservatives, build a new moderate base. But the electoral arithmetic indicated otherwise.)

The weakness of the moderate Republicans in presidential politics has been masked to some degree by the continuing ability of moderates, who control Republican Party nominations in most of the populous states of the Northeast and Midwest, to elect attractive governors and senators. The question remains, Why didn't Republican moderates organize themselves more effectively in the mid-1960s and later to regain a dominant voice in party affairs?

In retrospect, there are many possible explanations for the moderate Republican default in national politics. Successes at the state level created a kind of "star system" among the Republican governors and moderate "Wednesday Group" in the Senate and House. As then-governor (now U.S. senator) of Rhode Island John Chafee said when he assumed the chairmanship of the Republican Governors Association in the mid-1960s, "None of these guys wants to be the first one to pick up the telephone." Many of the moderates who owed their success to organizations and media campaigns directed by political consultants disliked the tough infighting of Republican national politics. Conservatives in Congress privately referred to the Wednesdays as "the soft-slipper boys." When a moderate like Rockefeller or Scranton did enter national politics, it was usually with a staff from his home state who made occasional sorties to Washington. For all practical purposes, the moderates were outsiders when it came to the politics of the Republican National Committee, House and Senate campaign committees, and, ultimately, the national convention. Moderate Republicans, who had never made a sustained effort to recruit, train, and place professionals of their persuasion in key organizational positions, forfeited any role in the administration of the Republican Party apparatus.

Those few young moderates who came out of the 1964 campaign were no match for the conservatives. When Republicans for Progress, a fund-raising organization of more senior moderates, and the Republican Citizens Committee of Eisenhower moderates folded, the young Ripon Society was left as the only moderate activist organization at the national level. After 1968, Ripon emphasized policy research rather than Republican Party politics. Nixon hired several key Riponites for policy and speechwriting positions in the White House as a symbolic gesture to counterbalance his conservative appointments. Other moderate staffers like Douglas Bailey and John Deardourff moved into the political consulting business, where they could work with moderate congressional and state candidates. But they were soon bidding for Nixon campaign and Republican National Committee contracts. The strategy of substituting Bliss for Burch gradually evolved into one of accommodation with Nixon. In the final analysis, there were neither the generals nor the committed troops for the protracted struggle that would have been necessary for moderates to regain control of the Republican Party. The conservatives' victory had given the Republican Party a permanent tilt toward the new Republican state party organizations of the South and West.

The Goldwater takeover of the party machinery was only the first step of the conservative strategy. Once the Republican moderates had been forced "to walk the plank," as Louisiana Republican Tom Stagg commented at the San Francisco convention, conservatives could turn their attention to consolidating the party. The excesses of the Goldwater partisans were forgotten as, with AEI in the lead, conservatism became respectable. Goldwater's heir, Ronald Reagan, ran a centrist Republican campaign for governor of California in 1966, similar to the campaigns of some moderate Republican governors in the East. An Eleventh Commandment, "Thou shalt speak no ill of another Republican," was designed to protect Reagan from the Republican defections that helped defeat Goldwater. In 1968 Rusher and White began to plan a far more sophisticated bid for the presidency, with Reagan as the new conservative candidate.

That the conservatives did not nominate and elect Reagan until 1980 was not because of a lack of power within the Republican Party. Nixon, using his personal leverage with party regulars and powerful Southerners like Senator Strom Thurmond, barely held off Reagan's challenge in 1968. White claims that only one or two Southern Republican delegations stood in the way of a Reagan nomination—indeed, Reagan aide Lyn Nofziger recently admitted that Reagan's California staff at the time fully expected to win. Nixon averted a serious conservative challenge in 1972, although in summer 1971, William F. Buckley, William Rusher, and a group of prominent conservatives known as the Manhattan Twelve, issued a statement of "suspension of support" for Nixon, and Congressman John Ashbrook mounted a largely ineffectual primary campaign. But Ford, using the full power of an incumbent President, stopped Reagan by only 1,187 to 1,070 delegate votes in Kansas City in 1976. Since 1964, then, the conservatives have either controlled the Republican nomination or been close to it. In the future, we can expect them to control the Republican Party nomination and probably to elect other conservatives than Reagan.

With the moderate Republicans more or less out of the picture, the conservatives have evolved what we might describe as a two-track nomination strategy. While preferring a true ideological conservative like Goldwater or Reagan, they can accept and work with party regulars like Nixon, Ford, and Connally. Sociologist William Domhoff, in *The Bohemian Grove and Other Retreats: A Study in Ruling-Class Cohesiveness*, reported that Reagan and Nixon used the July 1967 Bohemian Grove encampment to reach an off-the-record gentlemen's agreement on their participation in the 1968 nomination contest. Top Bush sources also report privately that Bush was selected as Reagan's running mate at a similar retreat in 1980. Bush and Kemp could well emerge as the next generation of Republican regular-conservative contestants. The range of candidates that receives serious consideration for the presidency has narrowed considerably since the 1960s, and been given a pronounced conservative tilt.

The career of Bill Brock is a good example of how the conservatives use the two-track strategy within the Republican National Committee. Conservative activists pressed for Brock's removal as RNC chairman after Reagan's election, because he was identified with the Ford wing of the party. Brock was replaced by Richard Richards, the conservative Republican state leader from Utah, and was subsequently appointed special trade representative by Reagan. Later the Reagan White House named Brock as its liaison with Republican House and Senate candidates in 1982.

Quite apart from control of the presidential nomination is the issue of control of party resources. Civics texts convey an image of our national political parties, based on the majority Democratic Party of recent decades, as weak coalitions of underfinanced skeletal or "cadre" state organizations that come together once every four years to nominate national candidates and write a platform. The Republican Party, however, at the time of the Goldwater movement, discovered direct mail and the small contributor. In 1981–82, the Republican National Committee, along with the House and Senate Republican campaign committees—each with highly developed direct-mail capabilities—raised approximately $167 million to spend on congressional candidates. The three comparable Democratic committees came up with only $28 million. The two parties also have vastly disparate operating costs. The Federal Election Commission gives 1983 annual budget figures of $160 million for the three Republican committees combined; compare this figure with the combined budgets of the three Democratic committees, roughly $24 million. (These figures may not be consistent with estimates used elsewhere in the text, obtained from different sources.)

Republican fund-raising success since 1964 has enabled the party to initiate a range of services to candidates and state party organizations. The party apparatus has become both the "giant service bureau" and the "central broker of information sources and computer programs" foreseen in my book *Parties: The Real Opportunity for Effective Citizen Politics* (1972). This machinery functions effectively as an adjunct for the conservative movement.

While some ranking conservatives like Rusher and Viguerie have pushed for a third-party movement, they have been pragmatic enough to use the Republican Party when it has suited their strategy. Conservatives fill many positions in the Republican Party structure. Viguerie-trained personnel move in and out of the various Republican direct-mail operations. New Right activists like Charles Black and Roger Stone have their own networks within the Republican and Young Republican organizations. Black, a former aide of Senator Jesse Helms, is credited by Alan Crawford as being the individual "most responsible" for the creation of NCPAC. After serving as political director of the Republican National Committee from 1977 to 1978, Black joined the Reagan presidential campaign. In 1982, Black and Stone organized the new lobbying firm of Black, Manafort, and Stone. Paul Manafort directed the 1980 Reagan presidential campaign in the South. *Congressional Quarterly* recently described a sophisticated nationwide public-relations campaign by the Senate Republican Conference, the official organization of all Senate Republicans, directed by Carter L. Clews, former director of public relations for the National Right to Work Committee. Clews was hired in early 1981 by New Right senator James McClure (R–Idaho), the new chairman of the conference. One of the clearest examples of New Right–Republican Party personnel interchange is Mark Tapscott, who recently moved from his position as publications director of the Republican National Committee to editor in chief of Richard Viguerie's *Conservative Digest*. Tapscott served as an aide to both Lyn Nofziger and former representative Robert Bauman before taking up his RNC post.

The Republican National Committee has used its resources to support a range of new activities to build a permanent Republican majority. A well-funded "Republican Journal of Thought and Action," *Commonsense*, was launched by then-party chairman, Bill Brock, in mid-1978. The quarterly, initially edited by Michael E. Baroody, son of AEI's William Baroody, Sr., has featured neoconservative intellectuals, many of them with AEI affiliations. Promotional copies of *Commonsense* were sent at considerable expense to the membership of the American Political Science Association. (The AFL-CIO has distributed a less expensive publication to APSA members on the legislative record of Congress. The only other organization affluent enough to do this is the Center for the Study of the Presidency, which periodically mails copies of its *Presidential Studies Quarterly*. Former Reagan campaign manager William J. Casey and William J. Baroody, Jr., of AEI serve on the center's bipartisan board of trustees.)

The RNC initiated another outreach program to the political science community, the Clearinghouse on Election Reform Studies. In 1981, the committee co-sponsored, with the DNC and the Kennedy Institute of Politics at Harvard, a conference on the parties and the nominating process. A full issue of *Commonsense* was devoted to the topic. Other RNC activities complement similar efforts of conservative organizations. The RNC has hired Reverend Donald Shea to work with groups on the political right. RNC ads for "Faith and Family" appear in the same Catholic publications that AEI has been cultivating for its research in religion and politics. One RNC unit is charged with developing and promoting "the new rhetoric," terms that will shape the political dialogue of coming decades to the advantage of conservatives in the same way the liberal rhetoric of the New Deal era favored the Democrats.

One final example of conservative-Republican cooperation is the career of Bryce Harlow, former congressional-relations aide in the Eisenhower White House, Washington lobbyist, vice president of Procter and Gamble, and behind-the-scenes conservative political operative. Harlow played an inside role in drafting the 1964 Republican Party platform. (The committee was chaired by then-representative Melvin Laird and controlled by Goldwater partisans.) Sixteen years later, Harlow, working with Michael Baroody, director of communications for the RNC (since appointed director of communications in the Reagan White House), was credited by Senator John Tower (R–Texas) as "the man who had a great deal to do with our report [the 1980 Republican platform] as finally written." Harlow tried unsuccessfully over several months to put together a Reagan-Ford 1980 ticket. One indication of Harlow's status in the Washington community is the Bryce Harlow Foundation, established in 1981 by 300 corporate representatives to honor the sixty-five-year-old lobbyist.

9
Conservatives and the Media: Equal Time

CONSERVATIVES seem obsessed by what they perceive as liberal bias in the media, and by the need to circumvent traditional channels to get their message across to the American people. Almost every conservative organization described so far has a publication or media program.

The public-relations programs of the conservative think tanks, notably AEI and Heritage, are perhaps the best examples of how the conservatives have successfully disseminated new ideas. Intellectuals associated with the think tanks are quoted regularly in the press or interviewed on television. The conservatives have established their own news syndicates, like the National Public Policy Syndicate in New York, which distributes policy commentary. Conservative organizations like the American Security Council and the Heritage Foundation have recruited senior news personnel. For example, Heritage's vice president is Burton Yale Pines, a former *Time* magazine associate editor and foreign correspondent who was also an AEI resident journalist before joining Heritage. The business media, particularly the editorial page of *The Wall Street Journal*, regularly present conservative ideas. So do other establishment media like *Newsweek* and ABC Television News.

The conservatives have also invested heavily in developing

their own media. The computer-based direct-mail operations of the Viguerie organization and Jesse Helms's National Congressional Club enable conservatives to mobilize single-issue constituencies. Conservative newsletters and magazines like *Conservative Digest* are directed to the faithful. Policy magazines and journals like AEI's *Public Opinion*, Heritage's *Policy Review*, and the RNC's *Commonsense* provide outlets for conservative intellectuals as well as material that can later be published in the establishment media.

Two new conservative newspapers have appeared in Washington during the past few years. The tabloid *Washington Weekly* was founded in 1978 by John P. McGoff of Panax Corporation and Reverend Lester Kinsolving, a conservative columnist, as an ideological alternative to *The Washington Post*. (McGoff, a business associate of Richard Mellon Scaife, had unsuccessfully tried to buy the failing *Washington Star* in 1974 and 1975; $11.5 million of his $26.5 million bid reportedly came from the South African government. Kinsolving lost his congressional press credentials for accepting payments from the South Africans.) *Washington Weekly* features Kinsolving's analyses of liberal bias in the Washington press and reprints columns by Patrick Buchanan, John Lofton, and Phyllis Schlafly, among others.

In spring 1982, the *Washington Times*, owned by the publishing arm of Reverend Sun Myung Moon's Unification Church, proclaimed itself a "conservative alternative" daily in Washington, D.C. James Whelan, former editor of the *Sacramento Union*, is editor and publisher of the paper, which in its first year had 150 editorial employees (60 from the Unification Church) and projected costs of $10 million. Some reports place the church contribution to the venture at between $12 million and $20 million. (Richard Scaife, it may be worth noting, is half owner of the *Sacramento Union*.) The new paper's executive editor is conservative columnist Smith Hempstone; associate publisher and general manager is Carlyle Reed, a former publisher for Copley News. The *Washington Times* has been a qualified success. By 1983 the paper's circulation had reached 130,000.

The alternative media being developed by the evangelical and business communities are also available to the conservatives. For example, Amway, headed by Jay Van Andel, acquired the Mutual Broadcasting System with its 950 affiliated radio stations in 1977. It has since purchased two major radio stations of its own, WHN in New York City and WCFL in Chicago. It has equipped its new network with a satellite programming capability. Reagan aide Edwin Meese III holds that the new American Business Network, or Biznet, "is going to revolutionize the way in which the business community can make itself heard." The Chamber of Commerce has opened huge new $6 million studios in Washington with a two-way communication feature for subscribers. Chamber president Richard Lesher calls Biznet, with its $2 million annual operating budget, the "business advocacy network." "Think of the increase in influence on the public-policymaking process," says Lesher, "when we have thousands of satellite dishes spaced around this country and we have real-time access to our members and they have real-time access to Washington." Coupled with the Chamber's direct-mail and telephone networks to constituency organizations and Citizens Choice, Biznet will be the most advanced political communications system in the country.

Smaller than the evangelical and business media but worthy of attention is the college conservative press. Since 1980, the New York-based Institute for Educational Affairs, the conservative educational foundation, has invested more than $100,000 in seed money to start or encourage some fifteen student publications. Among the recipients are the *Yale Lit*, the *Yale Free Press*, the

Yale Political Monthly, the *Harvard Salient,* the *St. John's Review,* the *Dartmouth Review,* Princeton's *Madison Report,* George Washington University's *Sequent,* and the *Stanford Review.* A range of corporations and conservative foundations back up the IEA. For example, the Scaife Family Charitable Trusts, the John M. Olin Foundation, the Dow Chemical Company, the Hunt Foundation, and individuals like Paul Mellon and Commerce Secretary Malcolm Baldrige have made well over $500,000 in contributions to the *Yale Lit.* Prominent conservatives and neoconservatives like William F. Buckley, Jr., George Gilder, Lewis Lapham, and Representative Jack Kemp frequently sit on the boards of these student publications or contribute articles to them.

In addition to AEI's independent television programming in public affairs, conservatives have also funded major PBS series such as Milton Friedman's *Free to Choose* and Ben Wattenberg's *In Search of the Real America.* PBS is the outlet as well for business programs like the *Nightly Business Report,* with regular commentary by conservative economists like Arthur Laffer and Alan Greenspan, initially funded by W. R. Grace and Cities Service. Business support for public television rose sixfold between 1973 and 1980. Oil companies like Mobil paid in full or in part for 72 percent of prime-time PBS shows in a sample week in 1981, causing some to suggest the network be renamed the Petroleum Broadcasting Service. Former CBS News president and journalism professor Fred Friendly said, "The corporations exercise a kind of positive veto" by financing and promoting programming of their choice, and other critics agree.

A relatively unknown but intriguing conservative organization, AMAGIN, Inc., of Erie, Pennsylvania, is heavily involved in independent programming. Billing itself as a "nonprofit national production company" and subsidiary of PBS station WQLN, AMAGIN (formerly Public Communications, Inc.) is headed by a conservative TV executive, Robert J. Chitester. Introduced by *Fortune* (February 1980) as "The Man Who Brought You Milton Friedman," Chitester is depicted as a "slightly eccentric," highly energetic, local TV executive who had tried unsuccessfully to produce several shows for the PBS network. In fall 1976, economist W. Allen Wallis, then chancellor of the University of Rochester and chairman of the Corporation for Public Broadcasting, introduced Chitester to the writing of Milton Friedman. Later, Wallis, a former colleague of Friedman's at the University of Chicago, arranged a meeting between Chitester and Friedman, who agreed to participate in a TV series. (Wallis was named Undersecretary of State for Economic Affairs by George Shultz in July 1982. He has served as a director of two network organizations, the Committee on the Present Danger and Ernest Lefever's Ethics and Public Policy Center). Chitester sought corporate and foundation sponsors as the "authorized merchant of Milton" and was soon rewarded by grants of $50,000 from L. E. Phillips Charities of Eau Claire, Wisconsin (followed by an additional $500,000 for *Economically Speaking*, a weekly show on economic issues produced by WQLN); $500,000 from the Sarah Scaife Foundation; $330,000 from Getty Oil; and $300,000 plus a full-page ad valued at $64,400 from the Reader's Digest Association. Ultimately, Chitester raised the full $2.3 million needed to produce the series and more than $500,000 for advertising and promotion.

With access to such funding, Chitester has produced or planned a series of TV productions on conservative themes described in his newsletter, *Communications & a Free Society*. The "Stan Freberg Federal Budget Revue," taking satiric aim at the federal budget, was aired on PBS throughout the week preceding the November 1980 election. Major funders included the Sarah Scaife Foundation, the Fluor Corporation, Mapco Incorporated, and L. E. Phillips Charities. A five-part series, *The War Called Peace*, studies "the true character of the Soviet Union and Communist ideology." A one-hour special, "Money and Medicine," examines new developments in health-care delivery resulting from market incentives. "Money and Medicine" was produced by Fleming "Tex" Fuller (who also produced the controversial documentary, "First Strike") on a $430,000 grant from the John A. Hartford Foundation of New York City. AMAGIN also produced an hour-long digest of the Fairmont Black Leadership Conference (organized by the Institute for Contemporary Studies in San Francisco) that debunked "the myth that black leaders are inevitably and inextricably tied to the liberal wing of the Democratic Party"; funding was provided by Melchor Associates and the Irving Foundation.

A number of more openly political conservative organizations are directly involved in what has become known as "advocacy television programming." The American Security Council, with a 1982 television budget of $5 million, leads the field. ASC's "The SALT Syndrome" was televised more than 2,000 times on some 500 television stations, in many instances just prior to Election Day. (ASC expects to more than recover the "several million dollars" invested in production, distribution, and purchase of air time, gaining over 1 million new contributors and $10 million a year.) The American Conservative Union's advocacy program on the Panama Canal was televised about 400 times and netted $500,000, which went to the lobbying effort against the treaties. Almost $1 million of The Conservative Caucus's $3 million budget goes to television projects, according to executive director Andy Messing, who has been involved with eight advocacy programs for a number of conservative organizations. Myron Berger of *The New York*

Times reported that at least two advertising agencies, Long Advertising in Miami and A. Eicoff in Chicago, now specialize in the distribution of advocacy programs. Two other agencies, Winner-Wagner in Los Angeles and Smith Harroff in Washington, D.C., concentrate on advocacy advertising and occasional full-length programs.

In the early 1960s only a handful of nationally syndicated columnists presented conservative views—James J. Kilpatrick, John Chamberlain, Rowland Evans and Robert Novak, and William F. Buckley, among others. To counter the "pro-Democratic, pro-liberal" bias among syndicated columnists, conservatives began to press for the equivalent of "equal time." Young conservatives were encouraged to pursue careers in journalism. Alan Crawford, in *Thunder on the Right*, chronicles the rise of several new conservative journalists, George F. Will and William Safire among more traditional conservatives, and Kevin P. Phillips, Patrick J. Buchanan, M. Stanton Evans, and John D. Lofton on the New Right. Evans and Novak have also increasingly aligned themselves with the New Right.

The new conservative columnists represent a change in American journalism in much the same way as the New Right representatives and senators represent a change in congressional politics. Like conservatives in Congress, their first allegiance is to the movement, rather than to their profession. They promote conservative policy ideas and provide commentary that support political objectives.

Besides cultivating and infiltrating the media for their own purposes, conservatives have developed an array of monitoring and pressure tactics. Sometimes the approach is indirect, such as the Institute for Contemporary Studies persuading Elie Abel to edit a book of essays, *What's News: The Media in American Society*, or AEI commissioning Michael Jay Robinson of George

Washington University (a contributor to the Abel book) to undertake a content analysis of network news programs. Other tactics are more blunt, like the recent Coalition for Better Television boycott of NBC. When one considers that Procter and Gamble (a conservative corporation that responded favorably to earlier CBT efforts and that keeps a tight rein on the story lines of its television soap operas) spent $650 million in 1980 promoting its products, the power of "market pressures" becomes evident.

Over the years conservatives have started a number of media monitoring efforts. Accuracy in Media (AIM) was founded in Washington in 1969 by Reed Irvine to expose liberal bias in the media. Besides issuing a bimonthly newsletter, *AIM Report*, the organization purchases stock in publicly owned media like *The Washington Post*, and confronts executives at annual meetings. AIM, for example, protested the *Post*'s lack of coverage of Communist atrocities in Cambodia when it devoted so much space to human-rights violations in Chile.

Another attempt—albeit a somewhat feeble one—to pressure an establishment newspaper to change its coverage is the "alternative to *The New York Times*" committee founded in June 1981 by the Center for the Survival of Western Democracies based in Riverdale, New York. Citing the "overwhelming cultural and political monopoly" of the *Times*, and its "pro-Soviet" news coverage, the group announced plans to develop "a national daily, adversarial to and competitive with *The New York Times*." One might be tempted to dismiss the group and its spokesman, Soviet émigré author Lev Navrozov, except that the committee members include Howard Phillips of The Conservative Caucus, William Rusher of the *National Review*, conservative columnist Ralph de Toledano, and Senator Jesse Helms.

The really big guns in the media monitoring effort, however, are corporate. Besides outright purchase, such as Amway's takeover of Mutual Broadcasting and the controlling Temple family interest in Time, Inc., and pressure through advertising, corporations have joined in media monitoring. We have already noted the role of Peter Grace at W. R. Grace. Chevron's public-affairs department has begun a series of Chevron Communications Research projects; a recent one was entitled "The Influence of Reporter Bias on TV Viewer Opinion" and featured field research by ASI Market Research of Los Angeles. Another project is a series of Focus Group Surveys to assess the effectiveness of the media presenting Mobil's image to the public. Above and beyond such individual initiatives is The Media Institute, funded by corporations and based in Washington.

Founded in 1976 as a public foundation, The Media Institute, a tax-exempt organization, was headed by the late Leonard J. Theberge, with a national advisory board including Bryce Harlow, then vice president of Procter and Gamble; Herbert G. Klein, former Nixon aide and now editor in chief of the Copley Newspapers; Henry Manne, Center for Law and Economics; Herbert Schmertz, vice president of Mobil Oil; Dale Vree, fellow, the Hoover Institution; Ronald Coase, editor, *Journal of Law and Economics*; and Murray Weidenbaum, who headed the AEI spin-off Center for the Study of American Business at Washington University in St. Louis before chairing Reagan's Council of Economic Advisers through 1982. A 1981 publication of The Media Institute lists a separate Board of Trustees including Theberge, Schmertz, and several corporate leaders like J. Robert Fluor and Raymond T. Bennett of Twentieth Century-Fox Film Corporation, as well as an expanded national advisory council. Patron memberships initially cost $500 annually; today they are $5,000 and above. Subscriber memberships, once $375 a year, are now $500. Although budget figures on The Media Institute were not available to me, a review of its literature, publications, and program announcements suggests that it is extremely well funded.

The Media Institute's major monitoring project is the *Television Business-Economic News Index*, a semimonthly summary of economic and business reporting on network evening news broadcasts, using abstracts from the Vanderbilt Television News Archive. A fund-raising letter for the institute cites survey data "showing that 95 percent of business stories on network newscasts were negative." An institute analysis for *TV Guide* found that TV news listeners get "a distorted picture of American business"; the institute's research and publications program attempts to counter such distortions. In September 1983, the institute published *Media Abuses: Rights and Remedies*, a handbook on communications law reviewing "administrative and judicial remedies available to individuals and corporations who are the subject of biased, distorted, or inaccurate media coverage." In a 1982 study, *Television Coverage of the Oil Crises: How Well Was the Public Served?* the institute concluded that television news virtually ignored basic economic forces such as the effect of supply and demand in its coverage of the oil crises of 1973–74 and 1978–79. Network news broadcasts relied on government sources for information on the oil crises 56 percent of the time, while independent experts outside government and the oil industry were called upon only 2 percent of the time. Government sources similarly dominated (77 percent) discussions of possible solutions. *The Wall Street Journal* greeted the report with an editorial, "Tunnel Vision on the Tube." A 1981 institute study, *Crooks, Conmen and Clowns: Businessmen in TV Entertainment*, took on television entertainment, charging that over half the corporate chiefs portrayed on television committed illegal acts ranging from fraud to murder and that 45 percent of all business activities shown on television are illegal.

In addition to these projects, The Media Institute has an ambitious program of research studies which are subsequently issued as institute publications. Tom Bethell, a former Washington editor of *Harper's*, who subsequently moved to AEI, prepared a study, *Television Evening News Covers Inflation: 1978–79*, concluding that an overwhelming majority of TV news stories tend to exonerate the government of contributing to the growth of inflation. Two institute studies on news coverage of nuclear power conclude that "the major television networks have injected, intentionally or otherwise, further fear—irrational, phobic fear—into an already fear-inspiring subject." *For the Good of Your Health*, an institute analysis of health and safety issues coverage, focuses on "the evolving relationship between the 'national' print media and Ralph Nader's Health Research Group." Future studies range from an analysis of the coverage of multinational corporations to a proposed review of coverage of business and economic affairs in selected large metropolitan areas beginning with Chicago and Pittsburgh.

A handbook on the media, *Who Are Those Guys? A Monograph for Business on the News Media Today*, was written by an old figure in the Young Republican/conservative network, John Fulton Lewis III, currently director of media relations for the American Farm Bureau Federation in Washington. Other projects that suggest the political clout and sophistication of The Media Institute include a business-media luncheon series addressed by, among others, Meese, Weidenbaum, and Antonio Navarro, corporate vice president of W. R. Grace, speaking on "Issue Advertising—A Corporate Voice in the

Public Debate." Speeches are published periodically in volumes entitled *Points of View*. Also of note is the institute's Economic Communications Center, which "provides the media free of charge with news analyses (and the opportunity to do interviews, including actualities) issued from economic experts immediately after a given development has transpired, or while it is breaking." The center's Committee of Economic Correspondents is drawn from lesser-known conservative economists in the network with a few "stars" like Arthur B. Laffer and black economist Walter E. Williams of George Mason University.

In November 1981, The Media Institute co-sponsored a one-day workshop, "Issues in International Information," in the State Department's East Auditorium, in cooperation with the American Bar Association's section on international law and Georgetown University's International Law Institute. (The American Bar Association Fund for Public Education has received some $1.4 million in contributions from Richard Scaife for programs described as "education against Communism.") The 150 participants were welcomed by then-undersecretary of state James Buckley, former Conservative Party senator from New York and brother of William F. Buckley, and addressed by assistant secretary of state Elliot Abrams, a former Democratic Senate staff aide and a prominent young neoconservative appointee of Reagan's. A two-volume set of the proceedings is available. Institute president Theberge earlier testified before a House subcommittee considering the International Communications Reorganization Act of 1981 on limitations on the flow of commercial information via satellites and computers across national boundaries.

Media Institute executive director Patrick D. Maines, writing in the institute's quarterly newsletter, *Business and the Media*, foresees enormous significance in cable, satellite, and computer technologies leading to "both the end of TV as we have known it and the beginning of a Golden Age in communications uniquely suited to the needs of a pluralistic and democratic country." While the revolution in telecommunications may be some time in coming, Maines points out that "the very environment in which these new technologies will operate is at this very moment a matter of intense debate among local and federal legislators, scholars and laymen, entrepreneurs and consumers." The Media Institute intends to play an active role in shaping the media environment of the coming decades.

The Media Institute has launched an impressive range of activities in a comparatively short time. Its innovative programs in comparative studies, international communications, and new information technologies point to the future orientation of the conservatives. In October 1981, the institute sponsored an international conference on media coverage of the energy crisis at Ditchley Park, near Oxford, England. Some forty journalists, business executives, educators, and government officials from the United States, Great Britain, France, West Germany, and Japan discussed how the media in their respective countries had covered oil and nuclear issues. Papers were commissioned from several participants, including Norman Macrae, deputy editor of *The Economist* (London) and a prominent figure in the growing international conservative network, and Alan Reynolds, vice president and chief economist of Jude Wanniski's Polyconomics, Inc. A book outlining conference highlights and making recommendations for future media coverage has since been published.

The international anti-Communist media strategy of the conservatives should not be overlooked. David Abshire, who heads Georgetown CSIS, has long been interested in international communications. Charles Z. Wick, a member of Reagan's "kitchen cabinet" and widely regarded as Reagan's best friend in Washington, was named director of the International Communication Agency after successfully managing an 85-city, closed-circuit TV hookup for the inauguration and attempting a similar effort to promote Reaganomics and raise funds for the Coalition for a New Beginning.

10

The Public-Interest Law Firms: Here to Stay

ANOTHER POLITICAL DEVICE created by liberals and copied by conservatives is the public-interest law firm. In the late 1960s and 1970s, the "Nader network" and some 100 liberally oriented public-interest law firms (including the Environmental Defense Fund, the Media Access Project, the Women's Legal Defense Fund, the National Prison Project, and the Natural Resources Defense Council) became a potent new force in American politics, combining strategies of litigation, research, public relations, and lobbying. The Ford Foundation alone contributed $21 million to ten of these firms from 1969–80. Leaders of the movement, who generally made substantially less than their colleagues in traditional law firms, emphasized that the young lawyers practicing "public-interest law" on behalf of the poor, minorities, consumers, and the general public were but a small counterweight to the thousands of corporate lawyers defending the interests of American business. A major objective of the movement was to build legal services and other activities begun by the new firms into the public sector, where they presumably had a better chance for survival.

In response, Ronald A. Zumbrum, an attorney who coordinated Reagan's welfare reform movement in California, and Roy A. Green, a former president of the Sacramento Chamber of Commerce, founded the nonprofit Pacific Legal Foundation (PLF) in Sacramento in 1973. PLF took up a wide range of welfare, environmental, and land-use cases, from a successful challenge of a government ban on the use of DDT against the tussock moth in the Pacific Northwest to helping to open Dulles Airport near Washington to the supersonic Concorde. The conservative business community, using the PLF as a prototype, then established the National Legal Center for the Public Interest (NLCPI). By the time Reagan assumed the presidency, NLCPI had set up some dozen conservative regional public-interest law firms across the country, the best known of which has been James Watt's Mountain States Legal Foundation. Meanwhile, PLF has flourished and as of 1982 was the largest of the conservative firms, with an 18-member staff, a $2 million annual budget, and offices in Washington, D.C., Sacramento, and Seattle.

The Mountain States Legal Foundation shows how the conservative organizations begin. Denver, the regional center of the resource-rich mountain states, was a logical site for one of the new firms. In 1976, Joseph Coors and NLCPI contributed $25,000 and $50,000 respectively of seed money to start the new organization. Coors retained Clifford Rock, a political consultant who had assisted him in setting up the Heritage Foundation, to undertake the initial organization and fund-raising for the Mountain States Legal Foundation. Rock raised the foundation's first-year budget of $194,000 and garnered pledges of several hundred thousand dollars from major corporations with operations in the West by mid-1977. (Scaife Foundation interests also contributed $355,000 between 1978 and 1980.) James Watt, a former staff aide of conservative Wyoming senator Milward L. Simpson—a U.S. Chamber of Commerce lobbyist and Nixon-Ford Administration official at Interior whom Coors knew through conservative circles—was recruited to head the foundation. Under Watt's leadership, it did battle with the Environmental Protection Agency, the Department of Interior, and liberal groups like the Environmental Defense Fund and the Sierra Club. By the time Reagan, with Coors's blessing, named Watt Secretary of the Interior, the Mountain States Legal Foundation had an annual operating budget of $1.2 million.

The liberal public-interest law firms foundered when the Ford Foundation stopped funding them. Liberal issues of the 1960s and 1970s have gone out of fashion. From the right, Howard Phillips, a former Nixon appointee to the Office of Economic Opportunity, has made "defunding" public-interest groups that receive federal support a priority target for conservatives. Meanwhile, as Raymond Momboisse remarked, "Pacific Legal Foundation is here to stay."

Not all conservatives, however, are content with the PLF-NLCPI model. The Scaife Foundation commissioned attorney and writer Michael Horowitz to evaluate the conservative public-interest law firms prior to the 1980 elections. The Horowitz Report, leaked to *The Wall Street Journal* in March 1981, concluded that conservative law firms, for all their funding, had "not generated anything like the organizational and intellectual force of their liberal counterparts." The report faulted the firms for not lobbying in the capital, concentrating instead on resource-consuming case-by-case litigation. Sensing the need for a more politically sophisticated response to the liberal network of public-interest lawyers, a group of conservatives turned to the Capitol Legal Foundation in mid-1980.

In its relatively short life, Capitol Legal Foundation (CLF), headed by conservative public-interest lawyer Dan M. Burt, has made a considerable splash. Its book, *Abuse of Trust*, charged Nader and his network of nineteen groups with misusing tax-exempt funds and other questionable practices. Burt has developed connections with New Right senators, joining with Senator Paul Laxalt to block the nomination of Nader associate Reuben Robertson to head the Administrative Conference of the United States, and with Senators Laxalt, Hatch, and Zorinsky to reopen the case of *Simer* v. *Olivarez*, involving the transfer of leftover fuel-aid funds to several liberal public-interest law firms. CLF participated in various Heritage Foundation transition projects and monitors several federal agencies, including the Environmental Protection Agency, OSHA, and the Securities Exchange Commission. CLF's activist stance was well illustrated by the vigorous nationwide campaign launched by Burt and his associates to promote their anti-Nader book.

Leslie H. Burgess, vice president of the Fluor Corporation and head of CLF's board, is credited by Burt for the initial funding and support of his foundation. Fluor contributes heavily (along with Exxon and Ford Motor Company) to CLF's projected $850,000 budget. The small foundation has enjoyed unusual media attention, including regular mention on the editorial page of *The Wall Street Journal*. Leonard J. Theberge, president of The Media Institute (which, coincidentally, is probing the media connections of Nader's Health Research Group), served on the six-member Board of Directors of CLF. Nader has welcomed the Capitol Legal Foundation's attack. "For years I've been trying to get people here in Washington to look at these right-wing foundations. They are really directly serving the interests of the corporations who fund them."

The Capitol Legal Foundation should not be confused with the Washington Legal Foundation (WLF), a New Right public-interest law firm founded by former Nixon Administration lawyer Dan Pompeo in 1976. WLF has initiated lawsuits on the Panama Canal and Taiwan Treaty issues, and was described in a Heritage Foundation newsletter as "the nation's largest (80,000 supporters) true Public-Interest Law Firm."

One other conservative public-interest law firm deserves mention: the Urban Legal Foundation in Oakland, headed by a prominent black lawyer, Tom Berkely, funded by corporate interests and advised by the Pacific Legal Foundation in Sacramento. By 1982, the foundation already had a staff of four, a five- or six-year development plan for four operational divisions (including litigation and economic development), and projections for national organization. The Urban Legal Foundation's guiding principle is that "discrimination is inconsistent with free enterprise."

11

Conservative Democrats and Libertarians: Alliances of Convenience

CONSERVATIVE DEMOCRATS and the Libertarian Party have a place in the new political order, although they are not part of the conservative network and differ from the New Right in some important respects.

One wing of the Democratic Party clearly serves conservative interests. Conservative Democrats are potential Republican converts in the House of Representatives, where they hold the strategic balance of power. Coalition politics in Congress, short of party realignment, is another possibility. The Jackson-Moynihan wing of the national Democratic Party is a counter to liberal "new politics" Democrats, keeping party nominees closer to the center. Conservatives would like to see the Democratic Party evolve "neoliberal" policies and candidates that accept the need for reindustrialization, reduced government spending and regulation, and "the new rhetoric" of a conservative Republican, business-dominated era.

We have already noted a number of attempts to further this goal: AEI sponsorship of Ben Wattenberg and Irving Kristol and their Coalition for a Democratic Majority and neoconservative intellectual networks; the AEI courtship of the American

Political Science Association; the Heritage Foundation connections to Daniel Patrick Moynihan and former Humphrey aide Max Kampelman. (Kampelman's lead article in the fall 1978 issue of Heritage's *Policy Review*, "The Power of the Press: A Problem of Our Democracy," later extracted in Viguerie's *Conservative Digest*, was part of the conservative offensive against the media.) A symbol of the conservative outreach to Democrats is *Commonsense*'s invitation to then-AEI resident scholar Jeane Kirkpatrick to write an article, "Why We [Democrats] Don't Become Republicans." (Kirkpatrick places herself among "traditional liberals" who have fought "to reclaim the Democratic Party from the anti-war, anti-growth, anti-business, anti-labor activists" who controlled the party under McGovern and Carter. Despite misgivings about Republicanism, she served as a Reagan adviser during the 1980 campaign and then accepted the UN ambassadorship.)

Prominent Democrats have collaborated with the conservatives in national security affairs. Two organizations in this field have played a significant role in public relations: the Coalition for Peace through Strength and the blue-ribbon Committee on the Present Danger. The Coalition is an American Security Council front organization with congressional and private sector co-leaders drawn from predominantly Republican, conservative, and retired military leaders. (A few conservative Democrats like Senator J. Bennett Johnston of Louisiana and Representative Richard White of Texas were among its founders.) Member organizations are all conservative, Republican, and émigré fringe (Cardinal Mindszenty Foundation, National Captive Nations Committee, Solzhenitsyn Society, Ukranian Congress, and so on).

In contrast to the Coalition, which emphasizes congressional membership, the Committee on the Present Danger (CPD), formed in November 1976, is an elite organization of some 193 individual members and an exclusive 21-member executive committee. The CPD membership reads like a *Who's Who* of the Democratic Party establishment (as well as a cross-section of conservative Republican leadership). More than twenty members, Democrats and Republicans, hold national security posts in the Reagan Administration. Billing itself as "wholly independent and nonpartisan," the CPD, a nonprofit organization, aims "to facilitate a national discussion of the foreign and national security policies of the United States directed toward a secure peace with freedom." Members donate their time. Charles Tyroler, a former director of Manpower Supply for the Defense Department, who ran the Democratic Advisory Council in the later Eisenhower years, directs the CPD offices in Washington. The organization's current $300,000 budget comes from 1,100 contributors, with a limitation of $10,000 per year per source. (Conservative financial angel Richard Scaife, also a member of CPD, presumably stays within that limit.)

Representative of Democratic establishment participation are former Treasury Secretary Henry Fowler, who chairs the organization along with C. Douglas Dillon, and AFL-CIO director Lane Kirkland, a member of its board. Max Kampelman serves as general counsel, and former Humphrey executive assistant William Connell is also a CPD member. Liberal and labor participants include Evelyn DuBrow of the International Ladies' Garment Workers' Union; Leon H. Keyserling, former chairman of the Council of Economic Advisers under Truman; black activist Bayard Rustin; and Albert Shanker, president of the American Federation of Teachers. Democratic hawks like Eugene V. Rostow, Paul Nitze, and Dean Rusk have been active on the CPD executive committee. Rostow chaired the executive committee (and was one of the forty-six CPD members who advised the Reagan transition) until his two-year tenure as Reagan's director of the Arms Control and Disarmament Administration. "We're in the business of educating the elite," says CPD director Charles Tyroler. The 14,000-name CPD mailing list of "opinion makers" includes 900 representatives of the press.

Andrew Kopkind, a political journalist of the left, argues that the Committee on the Present Danger, as an extension of the Coalition for a Democratic Majority, is a driving force behind "Cold War II" and "the leading source of organized opposition to several projects of detente diplomacy." But Kopkind underestimates the connections to the conservative network in the Committee on the Present Danger, which includes powerful conservatives like Frank R. Barnett, president of the National Strategy Information Center; W. Glenn Campbell, director of the Hoover Institution; William J. Casey, Reagan's campaign manager and CIA director; Ray S. Cline, former CIA official and number two at the Georgetown CSIS; John B. Connally; Rita E. Hauser, Nixon campaign aide and UN Human Rights Commission representative; and Professor William R. Van Cleave of the University of Southern California; as well as former Reagan aides Richard V. Allen and Martin Anderson.

If conservative overtures to traditional Democrats and Democratic hawks represent an attempt to change the direction of the party from within, the Libertarian Party is an effort to break up traditional party coalitions from without. Mark Paul remarks in a feature article in *Mother Jones* ("Seducing the Left," May 1980) that Libertarian publications like *Inquiry* have published well-known writers on the left. They play up the new party's anti-interventionist, antimilitary foreign policy and pro-civil liberties positions and deliberately camouflage its commitment to capitalism and free-market economics. Libertarian ideology leads to "the defense of a laissez-faire capitalism purer than anything that has ever existed in American history."

The rise of the Libertarian Party, a curious chapter in our story, further illuminates the complex origins of the new political order. In the late 1940s and 1950s, the Libertarian movement was composed primarily of intellectuals and free-market economists, including the so-called Austrian school of Ludwig von Mises. According to historian Russell Kirk, traditional conservatives, who emphasized the values of authority, family, and church, coexisted with Libertarians in the conservative movement. In the 1960s, the late novelist Ayn Rand and her followers (who include Alan Greenspan and Martin Anderson) gave Libertarian politics a new visibility. Then in the late 1960s, opposition to the Vietnam War and the military draft led to a split in the Young Americans for Freedom. The libertarian, antiwar, wing of YAF bolted and eventually formed the new Libertarian Party, founded in Denver in 1972.

In 1976, the Libertarian Party was transformed by an infusion of money from multimillionaire Charles Koch, then forty. "Until Koch opened his wallet," observes Mark Paul, "the movement was a ragtag collection of obscure academics, gold bugs, science-fiction nuts, and cranks." Koch family interests have invested more than $5 million since 1976, creating a new party apparatus referred to by some Libertarians as the "Kochtopus." Charles Koch, chief executive of Koch Industries, and heir of the estimated $500 to $700 million Koch family fortune in oil, chemicals, cattle, and real estate, is an MIT-trained engineer and mid-1960s convert to Libertarianism. His father, Fred Koch, was a member of the national council of the John Birch Society and a major contributor to right-wing and anti-union causes. The Koch Industries conglomerate, the fourth-largest family-owned firm in the United States, would, if public, rank 100 on the Fortune 500.

Koch has helped to fund a series of Libertarian organizations and publications and build a national leadership for the new party. The Cato Institute, founded in early 1977, is the main Libertarian public-policy research foundation—Koch's answer to the liberal Brookings Institution and conservative American Enterprise Institute. The major Cato Institute publication was *Inquiry*, a semimonthly political magazine that had been losing more than half a million dollars a year when it split from Cato to become independent in the fall of 1981. Cato also publishes a monthly review, *Policy Report*, and a quarterly, the *Cato Journal*. Other tentacles of the Kochtopus include the Students for a Libertarian Society (now defunct); the Institute for Humane Studies, a center for Libertarian scholarship (Austrian school economics) with an annual budget of $1.2 million based in Menlo Park, California; a monthly magazine, the *Libertarian Review* (which has recently been absorbed into *Inquiry*); and the Council for a Competitive Economy, a Washington-based business group devoted to the defense of the free market. The Reason Foundation in Santa Barbara, sponsored by Libertarian conservatives like William E. Simon, shades into the conservative labyrinth. It is regarded by Mark Paul as part of the Libertarian movement's right wing.

Meanwhile, the Libertarians continue to chip away at the Democratic left, nominating a gay Libertarian activist, John Vernon, for lieutenant governor of California in 1982. California Libertarians, who polled 5 percent in the 1978 California gubernatorial race, have in recent years convinced Eugene McCarthy, Nicholas von Hoffman, and Timothy Leary to address their conventions. McCarthy also wrote the introduction to the Libertarians' 1980 manifesto, *A New Beginning*.

David Koch—Charles's younger brother and the running mate of the Libertarians' 1980 presidential candidate, Edward Clark, a lawyer for Atlantic Richfield in Los Angeles—contributed $2 million of the $3.2 million spent on the campaign. Clark predicts that the Libertarians will be the majority party by the end of the decade, an optimistic estimate in light of the fact that he polled 920,000 votes in 1980. But Koch and company mean business.

12

Black Republicans: Playing by the Rules

THE CONSERVATIVES and the Republican Party, as part of their effort to form a new political majority, have solicited the support of racial and ethnic minority groups. Their largest and to date most successful achievement has been the building of a distinctly conservative black political movement. The civil-rights movement of the 1960s, the Goldwater nomination of 1964, and the welfare programs of the Great Society, kept black Americans firmly in the liberal Democratic coalition. Political scientists Norman H. Nie, Sidney Verba, and John Petrocik, in *The Changing American Voter* (1976), saw "the extreme and homogeneous liberal opinion profile of blacks" as the most distinctive new feature in American politics. Recent opinion polls show that blacks still strongly support public-sector programs in the face of a more general conservative trend. How do conservatives propose to overcome the deep political polarization and the liberal black leadership's almost total opposition to new conservative policies?

Black Republicanism in the early 1980s stems from two sources—the political or organizational black Republicans, usually from states with a tradition of moderate Republicanism, and a new breed of black philosophical conservatives. The first stream, represented by the outspoken anti-Goldwater National

Negro Republican Assembly of the mid-1960s, gradually aligned with the Republican organization during the Nixon-Ford Administration. By 1980, black Republicans had developed such groups as the National Black Republican Council, founded by San Francisco dentist (and former Reagan appointee as chair of the California Board of Dentistry) Henry "Hank" Lucas. Lucas, regarded as the black closest to Reagan, and Gloria Toote (a former Republican subcabinet officer and millionaire real-estate developer who seconded Reagan's nomination at Kansas City in 1976) were the two blacks to join the board of the Reagan political action committee, Citizens for the Republic, which has functioned as part of the conservative network since 1976, usually under the direction of top Reagan operative Lyn Nofziger. The organizational Republicans mobilized groups like Blacks Organized for Reagan and Black Voters for Reagan-Bush in the 1980 campaign.

The black population has always included cultural and religious conservatives. The network has simply identified them—as it has conservative intellectuals generally—funded them, and effectively promoted their ideas, which are supported by a minority within the black community. The undisputed star of the black conservative elite is Thomas Sowell, a senior fellow at the Hoover Institution and an economic historian who has published twelve books. Sowell, who is considered both brilliant and difficult (*Newsweek* refers to his "talent for bristling invective," while a *New York Times* writer notes that his "ad hominem approach to political analysis [has] provoked an intense negative reaction among many blacks"), is dismissed by some as an "ebony version of Milton Friedman," his former teacher. Yet Edwin Meese III, who addressed the Fairmont Black Alternatives conference organized by Sowell, Lucas, Toote, and the conservative Institute for Contemporary Studies in December 1980, credited Sowell and his black conservative colleagues with advancing "the ideas of the next ten years." Reagan has recently appointed two Sowell disciples, Clarence Pendleton, Jr., a former San Diego Urban League president, and Clarence Thomas, an assistant to Missouri senator John Danforth, the first black head of the U.S. Civil Rights Commission and head of the Equal Employment Opportunity Commission, respectively.

The basic ideas of black conservatism, as articulated by intellectuals like Sowell and economist Walter Williams, are limited government, free-market enterprise, and individual self-reliance. They view black dependence on federal programs, government, and grants from white liberal philanthropy as frustrating self-development and independent black leadership. Government-enforced minimum-wage standards, they claim, have increased black teenage unemployment. Government assistance and affirmative-action programs have stigmatized the majority of blacks, who would prefer to make it on their own. Instead, they believe the capitalist free-enterprise system offers blacks the best opportunities for advancement. Sowell is confident that the black masses, like other ethnic minorities, can pull themselves up by their bootstraps. While black liberals like Columbia's Charles V. Hamilton question the ability of free enterprise to redress the effects of racism in American society, black conservatism has obvious appeal to "resource-rich white conservatives who have never been comfortable with the black civil-rights leadership," as Lee A. Daniels of *The New York Times* points out.

The Hoover Institution has made its facilities available to Sowell, Lucas, and some 300 black conservatives who attempted to found a national mass-membership conservative black organization to rival the NAACP. The New Coalition for Economic and Social Change, now headed by Lucas, hoped for a direct-mail membership campaign to help support offices in various urban centers and a journal. In spite of initial funding of $200,000 from corporations and foundations (including Coors, Getty Oil, and the Olin and Scaife Foundations), the organization has yet to build substantial membership. The Heritage Foundation gave the coalition a boost, co-sponsoring and funding a Washington conference, "Rethinking the Black Agenda," in September 1982. The conservatives have also helped fund the Washington-based Lincoln Institute for Research and Education, founded in 1978 by J. A. Parker, who is still its president, and currently operating on a $300,000 annual budget.

The Lincoln Institute has all the trappings of a labyrinth organization. Its quarterly, the *Lincoln Review,* has featured articles by New Right senator Orrin Hatch and economist Walter Williams. Parker was one of a score of top-level conservative activists (including Viguerie, Schlafly, Dolan, Phillips, et al.) who met with President Reagan in February 1981. He has been active in Young Americans for Freedom since 1964 as a black conservative believing in "individual freedom"; been the host of a radio talk show; spoken on college campuses; and served as a Reagan volunteer in 1968 and 1976. Parker moved to Washington in 1970, established a consulting firm, and continued to function as part of the conservative network. His firm held symposiums on "free-enterprise zones," conducted a study of blacks and organized labor, and for a period represented the South African tribal homeland, the Transkei. He served as the 1980 Reagan transition team leader for the Equal Employment Opportunity Commission. The resulting "Parker report" contended that the EEOC had gone beyond the intent of Congress as stated in the Civil Rights Act of 1964, creating "a new racism in America in which every individual is judged by race."

Suzanne Garment's *Wall Street Journal* column, "Capital Chronicle," offered a revealing glimpse of black conservatism in April 1982, when she reported on a Lincoln Institute symposium, "Labor Policy, Minorities, and Youth." The audience of sixty blacks and whites was drawn from "the established right-wing network" and from others committed to free-market economics. The lead speaker, Anne Wortham, a black Libertarian, attacked civil-rights legislation for its violations of human rights. Others addressed the problems of the minimum wage and educational quality. Garment noted that the younger conferees, pursuing the time-honored American "political hustle," were betting on the heretical institute and the prospects of black conservatism. What especially marked this new group was that it had "learned to speak a new and different political language, the language of the corporate sector and economics and ideas like 'unintended consequences.' "

Lee Daniels likewise reports that the San Francisco Black Alternatives Conference was heavily attended by black business and corporate professionals who represent a new force among blacks. These people, trained in the nation's best business schools and employed by Fortune 500 companies, banks, and blue-chip investment firms, are searching for legitimacy in the black community. The black conservative ideology may give the black assistant treasurer of IBM, the black project manager for Bechtel, and the black senior vice president for Wells Fargo Bank a philosophical justification. Daniels foresees a "new black conservative leadership" emerging "from the nation's think tanks or the upper ranks of American business" in opposition to the liberal leadership of the civil-rights or affirmative-action organizations.

Representative of new corporate conservative blacks is Wendell Willkie Gunn, assistant treasurer of Pepsico and a follower of Sowell. In April 1982, he was appointed special assistant to the President and executive secretary of the Cabinet Council on Commerce and Trade. (Gunn's appointment, together with the promotion of Mel Bradley, former Reagan California appointee and Meese policy aide, to special assistant, was part of an effort to strengthen Reagen's standing with the black community.)

Pepsico is also the major funder of *Tony Brown's Journal*, a TV program on subjects of interest to blacks, which featured an unusual half-hour guest appearance by Ronald Reagan, discussing "The President and Black America," in February 1982. Another program questioned whether the government or community organizations can provide better social services for poor people. Pepsi began underwriting Brown, who subscribes to a philosophy of black self-sufficiency, with $225,000 in 1977, and now contributes approximately $2 million a year. The program is the most widely viewed black TV feature. Commenting to *The New York Times* on his success, Brown said, "When I first started someone said to me, 'Tony, money makes things happen.' I really didn't know what that meant. I heard the words. I just hadn't seen what I've seen in the last six years. Money does make things happen."

Another connection between corporate money and black conservatism can be seen in private sector alternatives to government programs. In addition to the Heritage Foundation's role in promoting urban enterprise zones, AEI has established a neighborhood revitalization project advisory council. In May 1981, AEI's black resident fellow Robert Woodson organized a two-day conference on "Urban Crisis: Can Grass-Roots Groups Succeed Where Government Has Failed?"

The religious right has reached out to blacks with a privately funded war on poverty. The project, the Foundation for the Poor, is a joint undertaking by conservative white Christians and businessmen. It is headed by black conservative Republican preacher Edward V. Hill of Los Angeles. Hill, pastor of the 1,500-member Mount Zion Missionary Baptist Church on the edge of the Watts district, was named one of the nation's seven "stars of the pulpit" by *Time* magazine in 1979. He also heads the World Christian Training Center, a Los Angeles–based organization designed as a model for coordinated action between affluent white suburban churches and inner-city congregations. The suburban churches provide money and job-hunting assistance for the inner-city unemployed. Hill has been an active member of the Moral Majority. The Falwell organization, Bill Bright's Campus Crusade, the Billy Graham Evangelistic Association, and at least half a dozen other large fundamentalist organizations back his private war on poverty, as do Clint Murchison, owner of the Dallas Cowboys, and Texas billionaire Nelson Bunker Hunt. In 1980, Hill headed the Black Clergy for Reagan Committee (although he still prefers the term "Negro"). He is a strong critic of the federal poverty program: "We don't believe it should cost $32,000 for every $7,000 delivered (to the poor) and we want to look at that process."

While black conservatism is on the rise, liberal black organizations are in decline. Liberal black leaders find it difficult to combat what they refer to as the "new racism" or "the new negativism" toward blacks and other minorities in the 1980s. In the 1960s, NAACP executive director Benjamin Hooks observes, "The consensus easily developed that it was a simple matter of right and wrong." But "you're not necessarily dealing with bad people anymore," concluded Congress of Racial Equality founder James Farmer. "You're dealing with people who don't agree with you." Charles Hamilton believes that the conservatives are "dead wrong" in believing that government action to overcome the effects of racial discrimination is no longer necessary. "But I don't see them as bad guys. They're coming from a philosophical base, and the burden is on those of us who disagree to take them on." Complicating the situation, "bad guys" like David Duke, the educated, articulate racist who heads the Knights of the Ku Klux Klan, have adopted the arguments of the neoconservatives and black conservatives against liberal affirmative-action programs.

Meanwhile, the Reagan Administration apparently sees no conflict between promoting black conservatism and policies that reverse the civil-rights rulings of the past. In a remarkable *Wall Street Journal* column in mid-April 1982, Norman O. Miller attacked "The Administration's Insensitivity to Black America." Miller was critical of some of Reagan's "bizarre and deservedly aborted appointments" to civil-rights agencies, the reversal of government policy on tax exemptions for private schools that discriminate, and the about-face of the Justice Department's civil-rights division under assistant attorney general William Bradford Reynolds. The liberal Leadership Conference on Civil Rights issued a 75-page indictment of Attorney General William French Smith's Justice Department, charging that it has "established itself as the focus of anti-civil-rights activity in the federal government." While most black Americans are resigned to a grim new era of race relations, conservatives feel they are in the best position to reshape black politics since the 1930s. When the economy improves, stated Republican National Chairman Richard Richards (who in 1982 welcomed a dozen black ministers from Maryland into the GOP and agreed to fund to the maximum at least four black Republican congressional candidates), blacks will rally to the Republicans once more. The message of Thomas Sowell and the black conservatives has been summarized by *Time*: "The American free-enterprise system has worked for every other group and is working for blacks who play by the rules."

13

How It Began:
No Immaculate Conceptions

THE FOCUS of *Ominous Politics* has been on what the conservatives have created. But I cannot resist speculating briefly about how and why they created it. The data gathered in the preceding chapters suggest to me a hypothetical model.

Conspiracy theories do not enjoy a good name among serious scholars. Still, both the left and right in America regularly employ them, identifying the Council on Foreign Relations, the Trilateral Commission, the Bilderberg conferences or Bohemian Grove encampment as the center of a plot to rule the world. Bertram Gross has dispatched all such efforts in what is probably the contemporary classic on the American establishment, *Friendly Fascism: The New Face of Power in America* (1980). Gross concluded that the establishment is "a complex of complexes, a far-flung network of power centers, including institutional hierarchies, held together by mutual interests, shared ideologies, and accepted procedures for mediating their endless conflicts." In Gross's view, "there is no single central conspiracy." Instead, he sees "situational logic" (in Karl Popper's term), rather than conscious planning, as the cause of events.

I wish to propose a third possibility, somewhere between conspiracy theory and situational logic. As the dean of Democratic Party chairmen, Neil Staebler, once observed, "There are no immaculate conceptions in politics." People make things happen. At the very least, they are the agents of situational logic or of social forces they may only partially understand.

I visualize the conservative New Right as a pyramid divided into three layers. (For this image I am indebted to Gross, who described three groups: leaders who provide strategic guidance, executive managers, and members.) I hypothesize that effective power rests with the leaders, a group of wealthy conservatives and corporate leaders who have funded it since its beginnings in the 1950s. While we know something about how elite politics functions at this level, we have relatively little hard information about how this group might have come together. (One of the advantages of money is that it buys privacy.) I will designate this as the conservative finance group. A more visible second tier of leadership, the executive managers, form what I will refer to as the strategy/operations group. Familiar names in the upper echelons are candidates for membership in this hypothetical group: W. Glenn Campbell of the Hoover Institution, Irving Kristol, William E. Simon, the late William Baroody, Sr., of AEI, Melvin Laird, and Richard Viguerie, among others. The third layer of the pyramid includes the majority of those visibly active in the network, especially the relative young or new faces who dominate the media—Terry Dolan of NCPAC, Howard Phillips of The Conservative Caucus, the Reverend Jerry Falwell and the electronic ministers, up-and-coming congressman Jack Kemp, the hundreds of conservative intellectuals —and form a network of subordinate communications and action groups.

The actual structure is obviously far more complicated than this approximation. Individuals like Jesse Helms and Paul Weyrich, who have built their own networks, cannot be categorized neatly. Visible conservative funders like Richard Scaife,

Joseph Coors, Justin Dart, and J. Robert Fluor, may also play an active role in operations.

The beginning of the conservative labyrinth as a conscious political development probably dates to the mid-1950s. (See chronology on p. 141.) A group of wealthy conservatives may have agreed to fund existing conservative organizations and develop new ones. At that time, small amounts of money could have a noticeable impact on poorly financed political parties and citizen action groups. The executive managers of the movement were probably involved by the late 1950s, and ran the Draft Goldwater campaign.

Conservative strategists may have hoped for a quick victory, if not with Goldwater, who began the process of political realignment, then with Reagan in 1968. It soon became apparent that public support for the New Deal was much deeper than conservative theorists like Milton Friedman had expected. The Johnson landslide and major extension of government programs to create the Great Society gave the New Deal an unexpected lease on life.

The challenge facing the conservatives—turning the country around—called for enormous political skill and sophistication. It required a sensitive appreciation of the dynamics of American public opinion, an intuitive sense of timing about shifts in underlying political attitudes. And it required money and lots of it, enough to seed and sustain the scores of organizations and operations needed to develop a new generation of conservative intellectuals and politicians who would redefine the issues and tactics of American politics.

In politics, conservatives focused on building an effective and durable governing majority. They have been fortunate in the political and physical longevity of Ronald Reagan, the surviving heir of the Goldwater era. Reagan's capture of the presidency was an essential first step in the conservative political plan; Republican capture of the Senate was at least as important. The Heritage Foundation "shadow government" monitoring the bureaucracy, and the continuing efforts to break Democratic control of the House of Representatives, are laying the groundwork for the steps to come.

Of course it is impossible to test this hypothesis. And it may be that the conservative infrastructure grew by chance and in response to unrelated forces operating in American society. Conscious planning may have entered the process later than I imagine. Leaders may have remarked on the independent existence of complementary groups and attempted to coordinate their work, rather than establishing such groups to work together.

Other observers, in short, may have different explanations for the development of the conservative labyrinth. But I would argue that this one has at the very least an intriguing plausibility.

FIGURE 2

Selected Events in the Development
of the Conservative Labyrinth

1952 Intercollegiate Studies Institute founded—William F. Buckley, Jr., first president

1954 William Baroody, Sr., becomes executive vice president of American Enterprise Association (later American Enterprise Institute)

1955 William Rusher and F. Clifton White take over the Young Republican National Federation

National Review founded by Buckley and Rusher

National Right to Work Committee founded

American Security Council (originally the Mid-American Research Library) founded

Lemuel Boulware (General Electric) hires Ronald Reagan

1959 Reed Larson joins National Right to Work Committee

1960 Glenn Campbell leaves AEI to head Hoover Institution

Young Americans for Freedom (YAF) founded at Buckley estate in Sharon, Connecticut

Richard Mellon Scaife funding of infractructure organizations begins (approximate date)

White and Rusher organize Draft Goldwater movement (through 1964)

1961 John Fisher joins American Security Council

1962 Rusher hires Richard Viguerie as YAF executive secretary

Georgetown Center for Strategic and International Studies founded by David Abshire and Admiral Arleigh Burke

1964 Baroody (AEI) and Campbell (Hoover) take leaves of absence to run Goldwater brain trust

Goldwater nominated at Republican National Convention in San Francisco

Republican Party initiates major direct-mail fundraising program

Major funding of ISI Weaver Fellowships begins

1965 Viguerie starts own direct-mail organization

Moderate Republicans back Ray Bliss, an organization Republican, against Goldwater Republican national chairman Dean Burch

Baroody changes AEI image to a more centrist "respectable" conservatism

Sarah Mellon Scaife dies; Richard Scaife assumes greater control of Scaife charitable entities

1965–66   Reagan gubernatorial campaign in California

Reagan promulgates the Republican Eleventh Commandment

1966–68   Melvin Laird and David Packard raise funds for AEI, Hoover, and Georgetown CSIS

Rusher and White work with Lyn Nofziger on Reagan bid for the 1968 Republican presidential nomination

1968   Richard Nixon nominated for presidency in Miami Beach in a three-way race with Reagan and Nelson Rockefeller; Rockefeller campaign for the nomination is the last major moderate Republican presidential campaign

Nixon elected; Laird and Packard appointed Secretary and Undersecretary of Defense

1970   AEI begins televised *Public Policy Forums*

1971   Joseph Coors decides to fund conservative political organizations

1972   Nixon re-elected; early phases of Watergate scandal
Laird leaves administration for Reader's Digest Association, maintains AEI affiliation

American Security Council moves to new "cold-war campus" in Virginia countryside

Jesse Helms elected to U.S. Senate; Tom Ellis and Viguerie organize the National Congressional Club

Institute for Contemporary Studies founded in San Francisco by Edwin Meese III and Reagan supporters (Scaife seed money)

1973   Pacific Legal Foundation founded by former Reagan aide in Sacramento (Scaife seed money)

Paul Weyrich and Edwin J. Feulner organize the Heritage Foundation; Coors and Scaife provide initial funding

Richard Scaife becomes chairman of the Sarah Scaife Foundation

R. Randolph Richardson becomes chairman of the Smith Richardson Foundation

Shadow Open Market Committee established to monitor Federal Reserve

1974 Nixon resigns; Gerald Ford assumes presidency

Federal Election Campaign Act of 1974 spurs creation of political action committees and direct-mail fund-raising

Business Roundtable founded

Laffer-Wanniski-Mundell begin supply-side economics

1974–75 Major New Right political organizations founded by Viguerie, Weyrich, Howard Phillips, and Terry Dolan; Helms aides John Carbaugh and Charles Black provide support

Richard Scaife tries unsuccessfully to buy *The Washington Star*

1975 Richard DeVos becomes active in the Christian Freedom Foundation

Viguerie founds *Conservative Digest*

Richard Lesher moves from Pepsico to head U.S. Chamber of Commerce

Irving Kristol publishes Wanniski article on supply-side economics in *The Public Interest*

1976 Ed McAteer joins the staff of the Christian Freedom Foundation

Charles Koch begins funding the Libertarian Party

The Media Institute founded (Scaife seed money)

The Institute for Foreign Policy Analysis founded in Cambridge (Scaife seed money)

Ford defeats Reagan for Republican Party nomination

Jimmy Carter elected President

Committee on the Present Danger founded

1977 Feulner becomes president of Heritage Foundation

Koch founds the Cato Institute in San Francisco

William Simon becomes chairman of John M. Olin Foundation

AEI begins publication of its own periodicals—*Public Opinion, Regulation*

Amway buys the Mutual Broadcasting System

Pepsico begins underwriting *Tony Brown's Journal*

Jay Van Andel organizes Citizens Choice for the U.S. Chamber of Commerce

1978 Republican National Committee publishes *Commonsense*

Lincoln Institute and Educational Foundation founded by J.A.Y. Parker in Washington, D.C.

Helms re-election campaign sets $7.5 million Senate record; Jefferson Marketing established to circumvent reporting to Federal Election Commission

1978–79 Major organizations of the religious right founded by McAteer, Robert Billings, and the Reverend Jerry Falwell

1979 William Simon, with Reader's Digest Association backing, publishes conservative manifesto, *A Time for Truth*

Argosy magazine taken over by the conservatives

John Connally hires Richard Viguerie, courts the New Right/religious right

The Heritage Foundation begins work on its blueprint for a conservative administration, *Mandate for Leadership*

1980 *Business Week* publishes feature issue on "The Reindustrialization of America"

"The Stan Freberg Federal Budget Review" and ASC "SALT Syndrome" broadcast on television the week before the election

Reagan elected President; Republicans win control of the U.S. Senate

14

Meeting the
Conservative Challenge

MANY LIBERALS expect Reaganomics and the conservative coalition to fall apart. They have unexpected support from conservative analyst Kevin Phillips, who observed that it was easy to predict that Reaganism, with its "patently contradictory fusion of monetarism and supply-side economics" and its vulnerable and volatile electoral coalition, would "unravel." But while liberals hope that a Mondale or Glenn Administration might replace the conservatives in 1984, Phillips outlined quite another alternative in his latest book, *Post-Conservative America: People, Politics and Ideology in a Time of Crisis* (1982).

"What kind of response can we expect from Reaganites committed to preserving a center-right political coalition?" Phillips asked. The most effective alliance between big business and the New Right, he argued, would be based "not on a nostalgia for free-market economics, but on a corporatist approach—something that could be called an 'Economic Security State.'" A corporatist state would require government management of capital and resources to promote economic growth, reindustrialization, and more favorable trade balances. The regime would protect the interests of "smokestack America" in the name of national defense, while simultaneously taking care of its middle-class constituency of farmers, wage earners, and pensioners. The politics accompanying and supporting the new corporatist state would involve "the radicalization of the electoral middle," which, Phillips observed, "tends to respond to cultural and moral traditionalism, nationalist pride and grandeur, and promise of national and personal economic security. Its slogans tend to be along the lines of 'Work, Family, Neighborhood,' and the like."

Phillips saw two immediate possibilities for the Reagan Republican Party. There is a chance that either the New Right conservatives will take over the Republican Party by 1984 or the New Right will form a new party. Helms would be the most plausible New Right candidate, drawing up to 10 to 15 percent of the total vote, mostly from the Bible Belt. Alternatively, the middle-American right might once again be part of a broader, conservative coalition "under a resurgent Reagan or another charismatic figure." Phillips foresaw "a peculiarly American authoritarianism, based in the Sun Belt and characterized by entrepreneurialism, high technology, nationalism, nostalgia, and fundamentalism."

What happens in the next few years depends in part on unpredictable developments tied to the word "economy." The weak recovery may be followed by another downturn, with unforeseen political consequences. The continuing budgetary crisis may precipitate a constitutional convention calling for extensive changes in the structure of government, a possibility the conservatives have both encouraged and prepared for. But in any scenario, one thing is clear: the institutions of the conservative network will help shape post-Reagan America.

How to respond is a question that the political center and left have barely begun to address. I use the term "center-left" to emphasize the importance of contesting the political center. The conservatives have been able to accommodate differences on the right and extend their coalition to the center. The center-left has much further to go in developing a common strategy.

We can acknowledge and support certain highly positive aspects of conservatism. First, the conservatives have made a substantial investment in the future of the American political system. The building of the network is itself a major accomplishment. Second, the conservatives and the business community have to their credit introduced a useful perspective into American politics and public policy. They show concern for the health of the economy, dealing with the welfare state, and achieving fiscal balance. Finally, there are legitimate national security, defense, and intelligence problems being addressed by the conservatives at the international level. We should view conservatism as basically constructive in impulse. While we may not share its vision of America, conservatism is committed as much to building the new as to replacing the old. One appropriate response, then, is selective support, acknowledging and endorsing those reforms that, to use a favorite conservative term, make "common sense."

Describing the labyrinth helps to identify it in the public mind, but that is not sufficient. It must be brought under public scrutiny and held accountable for the exercise of its power if it is to be accepted as part of the democratic process. Only an effective opposition can exercise this responsibility. The media can play a constructive role, especially through investigative reporting, but political opposition is more appropriately exercised by people in politics. Ultimately, only a stance that transcends both liberal and conservative positions can resolve the apparently fundamental differences that now separate us.

In the early months of the Reagan Administration, Richard Viguerie predicted that "the next few years will see a massive battle of conservatives and liberals to determine who governs the nation for the next three decades—and we've got a head start of years on them." Events indeed seem to be moving in the conservative direction, producing a dangerous imbalance in the political system. They have outthought and outplanned the liberals. It may well take the center-left the rest of the decade to restore the balance.

Liberals have reacted to the Reagan Administration by organizing a number of political action groups, think tanks, and publications. The response of Democrats in Congress, however, is essentially tactical and risks appearing negative and narrowly partisan. The leaders of the liberal coalition of past decades are growing older and are unlikely to spearhead a liberal counteroffensive. And a distressing number of younger liberal politicians are so-called neoliberals who seem all too willing to adopt the rhetoric of the conservatives—which means accepting conservative definitions of what the problems are.

It is time that the center-left articulated its own response. The developments I have described require a response that goes beyond traditional Democratic Party politics. Substantial resources and groups are available to create a prospective center-left coalition. They include:

- the core institutions of the old liberal–labor–civil-rights coalition, including the generation of leaders that developed in the 1960s and 1970s

- the liberal intelligentsia in the universities and major urban centers, who should be able to counterbalance at least partially the financial resource advantages of the conservatives through intelligent action, i.e., working "smart"

- the moral legacy of the civil-rights movement and the powerful ideal of a multiracial society that advances social justice and unifies rather than divides American society

- the women's movement, perhaps the most significant political force of the last third of this century—effectively excluded from Reagan conservatism

- moderate and liberal Republicans in the Congress, strategic industrial states, and the business and professional communities

- allies within the corporate power structure who would assume more social responsibility than is represented by Friedmanism or neoconservatism

- a new socially humane, post-Keynesian economics of the center-left that addresses the realities of American capitalism, including its economic power

- the public demand for a sensible arms control and disarmament strategy, exemplified by the widespread, spontaneous support for a nuclear freeze

- the great, largely unorganized constituency for the defense of the Constitution and constitutional values against radical political change

- the leaders of and participants in the other political movements that came of age in the 1960s and 1970s—the anti-Vietnam War movement, the consumer and environmental movements, the racial and sexual minorities, the elderly, the handicapped, and so on

- the cultural alternative force represented by the "counterculture" and youth movements of the 1960s and since—including the human potential/consciousness movement and New Age politics

- global citizen "networking" and organization that transcends the nationalist, militarist focus of the conservative movement and the elite character of its current international contacts

- the widespread support for an American foreign policy that advances democratic values and social justice, most noticeably in Latin America, where reform elements in the Roman Catholic Church have made an unusual public stand

- the potential for participatory, interactive democratic politics presented by information technology and communications media; cable television, personal computer networking, satellite relays, and so on (the telephone still provides one of the most powerful tools and models for democratic politics)

- the commitment of the overwhelming majority of professionals in the communications media to the values of democratic as opposed to a technocratic, manipulative politics

- financial resources that include both traditional sources (wealthy contributors, labor unions, liberal foundations, some corporations) and the affluent, socially committed young professionals of the middle class

Putting together a coalition of the center-left is a formidable task for the political generation trained and tested in the 1960s and 1970s. Yet, only as we learn to put aside internal disagreements and differences in goals and function together as worthy opponents to the conservatives will we earn the opportunity to lead America to the realization of a broader vision.

Abbreviations Used in Text

AAUCG	Americans Against Union Control of Government
ABA	American Bar Association
ACSH	American Council on Science and Health
ACU	American Conservative Union
AEI	American Enterprise Institute
AIM	Accuracy in Media
ALEC	American Legislative Exchange Council
APF	American Political Foundation
APSA	American Political Science Association
ASC	American Security Council
BIPAC	Business/Industry Political Action Committee
CBN	Christian Broadcast Network
CBT	Coalition for Better Television
CED	Committee for Economic Development
CEO	Chief Executive Officer
CFF	Christian Freedom Foundation
CLF	Capitol Legal Foundation
CPD	Committee on the Present Danger
CQ	*Congressional Quarterly*
CSFC	Committee for the Survival of a Free Congress
CSIS	Center for Strategic and International Studies (Georgetown University)
DNC	Democratic National Committee
DSG	Democratic Study Group
FACS	Foundation for American Communications
FEC	Federal Election Commission
FPA	Family Protection Act
IAM	International Association of Machinists
IAR	Institute of American Relations

ICS	Institute for Contemporary Studies
IEA	Institute for Educational Affairs
IFPA	Institute for Foreign Policy Analysis
ISC	Institute for the Study of Conflict
ISI	Intercollegiate Studies Institute
L&EC	Law & Economics Center (Emory University)
NAM	National Association of Manufacturers
NCEC	National Committee for an Effective Congress
NCPAC	National Conservative Political Action Committee
NLCPI	National Legal Center for the Public Interest
NPLPAC	National Pro-Life Political Action Committee
NRTWC	National Right to Work Committee
PAC	Political Action Committee
PBS	Public Broadcasting Service
PLF	Pacific Legal Foundation
PSRC	Public Service Research Council
PTL	People That Love (Praise The Lord)
RAVCO	Richard A. Viguerie Company
RNC	Republican National Committee
WLF	Washington Legal Foundation
YAF	Young Americans for Freedom
YRNF	Young Republican National Federation

Selected References

Chapter 1

"The Conservative Network: How It Plans to Keep on Winning," *U.S. News & World Report,* July 20, 1981, pp. 46–50.

Dan Morgan, "Conservatives: A Well-Financed Network," *The Washington Post,* January 4, 1981, pp. A1, A14.

"Neoconservatism: An Idea Whose Time is Now," *Esquire,* February 13, 1979.

Chapter 2

W. E. Barnes, "Slick Reply to Anti-smoking Proposal," *San Francisco Examiner,* August 31, 1978, pp. A1, A8, A10.

Sidney Blumenthal, "The Right Idea: Washington's Conservative Think Tanks," *The Boston Globe Magazine,* August 8, 1982 (profiles of AEI and Heritage).

Dom Bonafede, "Public Policy Report: Issue-Oriented Heritage Foundation Hitches Its Wagon to Reagan's Star," *National Journal,* March 20, 1982, pp. 502–7.

"The Hoover Institution Edges Toward the Middle," *Business Week,* August 1982, pp. 118, 122.

Morton Kondracke, "The Heritage Model," *The New Republic,* December 20, 1980.

James Lardner, "Thick and Think Tank: David Abshire's CSIS Ponders Policy with Kissinger and Fred Flintstone," *The Washington Post,* September 21, 1982.

Joanne Omang, "The Heritage Report: Getting the Government Right with Reagan," *The Washington Post,* November 16, 1980, p. A6.

Peter H. Stone, "Conservative Brain Trust," *The New York Times Magazine,* May 17, 1981 (profile of American Enterprise Institute).

Dennis A. Williams, et al., "Idea Factories of the Right," *Newsweek,* December 1, 1980, pp. 35–36.

Jim Wood, "A Think Tank That Acts," *San Francisco Examiner,* January 4, 1981, p. A1 (profile of Institute of Contemporary Studies).

Chapter 3

Stephen K. Beckner, "Rep. Newt Gingrich: A New Conservative Leader for the 80s," *Conservative Digest,* May 1982, pp. 6–11.

Lindley H. Clark, Jr., "The Monetarist: Karl Brunner Sways Government Policies, Rides Herd on the Fed," *The Wall Street Journal,* October 7, 1981, pp. 1, 17.

Mark Dowie, "The Bechtel File: How the Master Builders Protect Their Beachheads," *Mother Jones,* September/October 1978, pp. 28–38.

"The Free World of Private Companies," *Dun's Review,* September 1978, pp. 57–64.

Thomas C. Hayes, "Bechtel: A Reclusive Giant: Shultz Move Puts Spotlight on Builder," *The New York Times,* July 8, 1982, pp. D1, D6.

Henri Lepage, *Tomorrow, Capitalism: The Economics of Economic Freedom* (La Salle, Ill.: Open Court, 1982).

Thomas Lueck, "Bechtel and Its Links to Reagan: Reclusive Owner Issues Note on Ethics," *The New York Times,* December 5, 1980, pp. D1, D3.

Walter McQuade, "Bob Fluor, Global Superbuilder," *Fortune,* February 26, 1979, pp. 54–61.

Lisa Miller Mesdag, "The 50 Largest Private Industrial Companies," *Fortune,* May 31, 1982, pp. 108–14.

"Reaganomics Under Review," *The Wall Street Journal,* March 22, 1982, p. 28 (editorial).

Karen Rothmyer, "Citizen Scaife," *Columbia Journalism Review,* July/August 1981, pp. 41–50; reprinted as "The Mystery Angel of the New Right," *The Washington Post,* July 12, 1981 pp. C1, C4.

Harold Seneker with Jonathan Greenberg and John Dorfman, "The Forbes Four Hundred: The Richest People in America," *Forbes,* September 13, 1982.

David Warner, "Scaife: Financier of the Right," *Pittsburgh Post-Gazette,* April 20, 1981.

Chris Welles, "The Supply-Side 'Cabal,'" *Esquire,* August 1981.

WGBH-TV, "Nova: Cobalt Blues," November 1982.

Chapter 4

Americans for Democratic Action, *A Citizen's Guide to the Right Wing* (Washington, D.C.: Americans for Democratic Action, 1978).

Dom Bonafede, "Political Report: Part Science, Part Art, Part Hokum, Direct Mail Now a Key Campaign Tool," *National Journal,* July 31, 1982, pp. 1332–36.

Alan Crawford, *Thunder on the Right: The "New Right" and the Politics of Resentment* (New York: Pantheon, 1980).

E. J. Dionne, Jr., "Mail-Order Campaigners," *The New York Times,* September 7, 1980, p. 9.

"The Far Right Wing" (special issue), *Viewpoint: An IUD Quarterly* 8, no. 2, Second Quarter, 1978.

J. Regan Kerney, "The Cold-War Campus," *The Washington Post,* January 8, 1979, p. C1.

Sue Mullin, "Marshner: Irish Fire on the Right," *The Washington Times,* July 27, 1982, pp. 1B, 2B.

Peter Ross Range, "Inside the New Right War Machine," *Playboy,* August 1981.

Perry Deane Young, *God's Bullies: Native Reflections on Preachers and Politics* (New York: Holt, Rinehart and Winston, 1982).

Chapter 5

Dudley Clendinen, "Christian New Right's Rush to Power," *The New York Times,* August 18, 1980, p. B7 (second of four articles on the rise of ultraconservative evangelical Christians as a political force).

Flo Conway and Jim Siegelman, *Holy Terror: The Fundamentalist War on America's Freedoms in Religion, Politics and Our Private Lives* (New York: Doubleday, 1982).

Maxwell Glen, "The Electronic Ministers Listen to the Gospel According to the Candidates," *National Journal,* December 22, 1979.

Johnny Green, "The Astonishing Wrongs of the New Moral Right," *Playboy,* January 1981.

Alan and Marc Levin, "Crisis to Crisis: Portrait of an American Zealot" (transcript of PBS broadcast, July 30, 1982).

Thomas B. Mechling, "Special Report: Amway's 'Gold Dust

Twins,'" *Interchange* (Newsletter of Interchange Resource Center), 1980.

Marguerite Michaels, "Billy Graham: America Is Not God's Only Kingdom," *Parade*, February 1, 1981.

"Mobilizing the Moral Majority," *Conservative Digest*, August 1979.

Jeremy Rifkin with Ted Howard, *The Emerging Order: God in the Age of Scarcity* (New York: Putnam, 1979).

"Roundtable's President Ed McAteer Is Music Man of Religious Right," *Conservative Digest*, January 1981.

Lynda Schuster, "Latin Revival: Central American Gains by Evangelicals Reflect Rising Political Unrest," *The Wall Street Journal*, December 7, 1982, pp. 1, 22.

Kenneth L. Woodward, "The Split-Up Evangelicals," *Newsweek*, April 26, 1982.

Chapter 6

Ann Crittenden, "The Economic Wind's Blowing Toward the Right—For Now," *The New York Times*, July 16, 1978, Section 3, pp. 1, 9.

Greg Denier, "Corporate Political Movement" (speech, January 15, 1980).

Walter Guzzardi, Jr., "Judges Discover the World of Economics," *Fortune*, May 21, 1979, pp. 58–66.

Walter Issacson, "Running with the PACs: How Political Action Committees Win Friends and Influence Elections," *Time*, October 25, 1982, pp. 20–26.

Richard I. Kirkland, Jr., "Fat Days for the Chamber of Commerce," *Fortune*, September 21, 1981, pp. 144–57.

Douglas Martin, "Labor Nemesis: When the Boss Calls in This Expert, the Union May Be in Real Trouble," *The Wall Street Journal*, November 19, 1979, pp. 1, 22.

Thomas B. Mechling, "Business Fronts of the Far Far Right," *Business and Society Review*, Summer 1978, pp. 32–37 (profile of the National Right to Work Committee).

Herbert E. Meyer, "The Decline in Strikes," *Fortune*, November 21, 1981, pp. 66–70.

Norman Podhoretz, "The New Defenders of Capitalism," *Harvard Business Review*, March/April 1981.

Sally Quinn, "Herb Schmertz, Kennedy's Mobil Superflack," *The Washington Post*, November 28, 1979, pp. B1, B3.

Stephen J. Sansweet, "PAC Pressure? Political-Action Units at Firms are Assailed by Some Over Tactics," *The Wall Street Journal*, July 24, 1980.

Leonard and Mark Silk, *The American Establishment* (New York: Basic Books, 1980).

"The Swarming Lobbyists," *Time*, August 7, 1978, pp. 14–22.

David Warsh, "The Long Genesis of Reaganomics," *San Francisco Chronicle*, January 19, 1981.

Chapter 7

David S. Broder, "Republicans Crank Up Computers for Battles over Redistricting," *The Washington Post*, March 10, 1981, pp. A1, A6.

"The Helms Network," *Congressional Quarterly*, Weekly Report, No. 10, March 6, 1982, pp. 499–595.

"Kemp's Political Game Plan," *Business Week*, May 18, 1981, p. 167.

"The Right in Congress: Seeking a Strategy," *Congressional Quarterly*, Weekly Report, No. 31, August 5, 1978, pp. 2022–28.

"To the Right March: Jesse Helms is the New Right's Righteous Warrior and His Battle is Nigh"; "Seeking Strategy on Social Issues"; and "The Machine that Jesse Built," *Time*, September 14, 1981, pp. 24–39.

Chapter 8

Dennis Farney, "GOP Jeopardy: Republican Candidates in Midwest Face Perils of Races in Recession," *The Wall Street Journal*, April 13, 1982, pp. 1, 22.

"GOP to Stress 'Demo Failures,' " *The Palm Beach Post*, January 31, 1982, p. A18.

Nicholas Lemann, "The Conservative Road," *The Washington Post*, February 22–24, 1981 (three-part series).

"Republican Groups Tap Smaller Donors to Outdo Democrats," *The Wall Street Journal,* October 8, 1982, p. 6.

Martin Schramm, "GOP Meets Reality—on the Button," *The Washington Post,* May 16, 1982, pp. A1, A4, A5.

"Senate Republicans Using Incumbency to Advantage in Snappy Media Operation," *Congressional Quarterly,* Weekly Report, No. 23, June 6, 1981, pp. 993–95.

Chapter 9

Myron Berger, "Advocacy Programs—Social Action Groups Are Wielding a Powerful Weapon," *The New York Times,* May 24, 1981, pp. 27, 35.

Peter W. Bernstein, "The Man Who Brought You Milton Friedman," *Fortune,* February 25, 1980, pp. 108–112.

Blaine Harden, "Robert L. Bartley, *Wall Street Journal* Editor: His Crusade to Turn America Right," *The Washington Post Magazine,* July 11, 1982.

Charlotte Hays, "Media: Taking on *The Washington Post: The Washington Times* Seems Willing to Pay Any Price to Give the City a Conservative Voice and a Second Paper," *The Washingtonian,* July 1982.

William A. Henry, "Conservative Rebels on Campus: Student Editors and Their Papers Are Ready on the Right," *Time,* November 8, 1982, pp. 80, 82.

James Lardner, "The Tug of Words over Yale's 'Lit,'" *The Washington Post,* November 25, 1982, pp. D1, D21.

Jane Mayer, "Survival Tactics: Cuts in Federal Aid Lead Public TV to Try a Bit of Free Enterprise," *The Wall Street Journal,* March 10, 1982, pp. 1, 20.

Dan Morgan, "Getting Our Ideology in *The Wall Street Journal,*" *The Washington Post,* February 15, 1981, pp. C1, C5.

Chapter 10

Margot Hornblower, "Conservative Winds Reshaping Public Interest Law," *The Washington Post,* January 14, 1980, p. A3.

"The Horowitz Report," *The Wall Street Journal,* March 19, 1981, p. 26.

Tom Nicholson, "Ralph Nader: An 'Abuse of Trust'?" *Newsweek,* April 19, 1982.

Ron Wolf, "The High Road to Power: James Watt, the Tough Evangelical in Charge of Interior," *Rocky Mountain Magazine,* March/April 1981.

Chapter 11

Andrew Kopkind, "Cold War II," *New Times,* October 30, 1978, pp. 28–41.

Mark Paul, "Seducing the Left: The Third Party That Wants You," *Mother Jones,* May 1980, pp. 47–49, 60–62.

Jerry Roberts, "The Right Wing Theorists: A Republican Underground," *San Francisco Chronicle,* February 2, 1981.

Stephen Wermiel, "Libertarian Ed Clark Has One Main Idea: Cut Big Government," *The Wall Street Journal,* September 26, 1980, pp. 1, 26.

Curtis Wilkie, "Their Mission Is to Keep 'Strength on the Barricades,'" *The Boston Globe,* April 28, 1981 (profile of the Committee on the Present Danger).

Chapter 12

Russell Chandler, "Waging a Private War on Poverty," *San Francisco Chronicle,* April 7, 1981, p. 18.

Lee A. Daniels, "The New Black Conservatives," *The New York Times Magazine,* October 4, 1981.

Herbert H. Denton, "Administration-Inspired Black Group Admits Early Progress Has Been Slow," *The Washington Post,* September 14, 1982, p. A2.

C. Gerald Fraser, "*Tony Brown's Journal* Endures," *The New York Times,* February 7, 1982.

Suzanne Garment, "Capital Chronicle: Lincoln Heretics Preach and Praise Black Conservatism," *The Wall Street Journal,* April 9, 1982, p. 22.

William A. Henry III, "Sowell on the Firing Line," *Time,* August 24, 1981, p. 25.

Manning Marable, "Black Reaganism: A Rogues Gallery," *Washington, D.C. Afro-American,* April 24, 1982.

Norman C. Miller, "The Administration's Insensitivity to Black America," *The Wall Street Journal,* April 15, 1982, p. 28.

Tom Morganthau, et al., "The Black Conservatives," *Newsweek,* March 9, 1981, pp. 29–33.

"National Report: Sowell and His Supporters Win Key Posts from Reagan," *Jet,* April 26, 1982, p. 5.

Eleanor Randolph, "The Black Fears of a 'New Racism,'" *San Francisco Sunday Examiner & Chronicle,* January 6, 1980, p. 26.

Jacqueline Trescott, "Sudden Spotlight on Black Republicans," *San Francisco Chronicle,* November 28, 1980.

Chapter 13

Bertram M. Gross, *Friendly Fascism: The New Face of Power in America* (New York: M. Evans, 1980).

Chapter 14

Kevin P. Phillips, *Post-Conservative America: People, Politics and Ideology in a Time of Crisis* (New York: Random House, 1982).

Index